CIA and the
Wars in Southeast Asia

1947–75

Selections, introduction, and summaries
by Clayton D. Laurie, CIA Historian,
and Andres Vaart, Managing Editor

August 2016

CENTER *for the* STUDY *of* INTELLIGENCE

Mission   The mission of *Studies in Intelligence* is to stimulate within the Intelligence Community the constructive discussion of important issues of the day, to expand knowledge of lessons learned from past experiences, to increase understanding of the history of the profession, and to provide readers with considered reviews of public media concerning intelligence.

The journal is administered by the Center for the Study of Intelligence, which includes the CIA's History Staff, CIA's Lessons Learned Program, and the CIA Museum. In addition, it houses the Emerging Trends Program, which seeks to identify the impact of future trends on the work of US intelligence.

Contributions   *Studies in Intelligence* welcomes articles, book reviews, and other communications. Hardcopy material or data discs (preferably in .doc or .rtf formats) may be mailed to:

Editor
Studies in Intelligence
Center for the Study of Intelligence
Central Intelligence Agency
Washington, DC 20505

Awards   The Sherman Kent Award of $3,500 is offered annually for the most significant contribution to the literature of intelligence submitted for publication in *Studies*. The prize may be divided if two or more articles are judged to be of equal merit, or it may be withheld if no article is deemed sufficiently outstanding. An additional amount is available for other prizes.

Another monetary award is given in the name of Walter L. Pforzheimer to the graduate or undergraduate student who has written the best article on an intelligence-related subject.

Unless otherwise announced from year to year, articles on any subject within the range of *Studies'* purview, as defined in its masthead, will be considered for the awards. They will be judged primarily on substantive originality and soundness, secondarily on literary qualities. Members of the Studies Editorial Board are excluded from the competition.

The Editorial Board welcomes readers' nominations for awards.

Dedication

This volume is dedicated to the men and women of the United States, Allied nations, and peoples of the region with whom US intelligence worked to thwart the advance of communism in Southeast Asia. Among the more than fifty-eight thousand Americans who gave their lives were eighteen members of the Central Intelligence Agency, their sacrifices marked by stars carved into CIA's Memorial Wall.

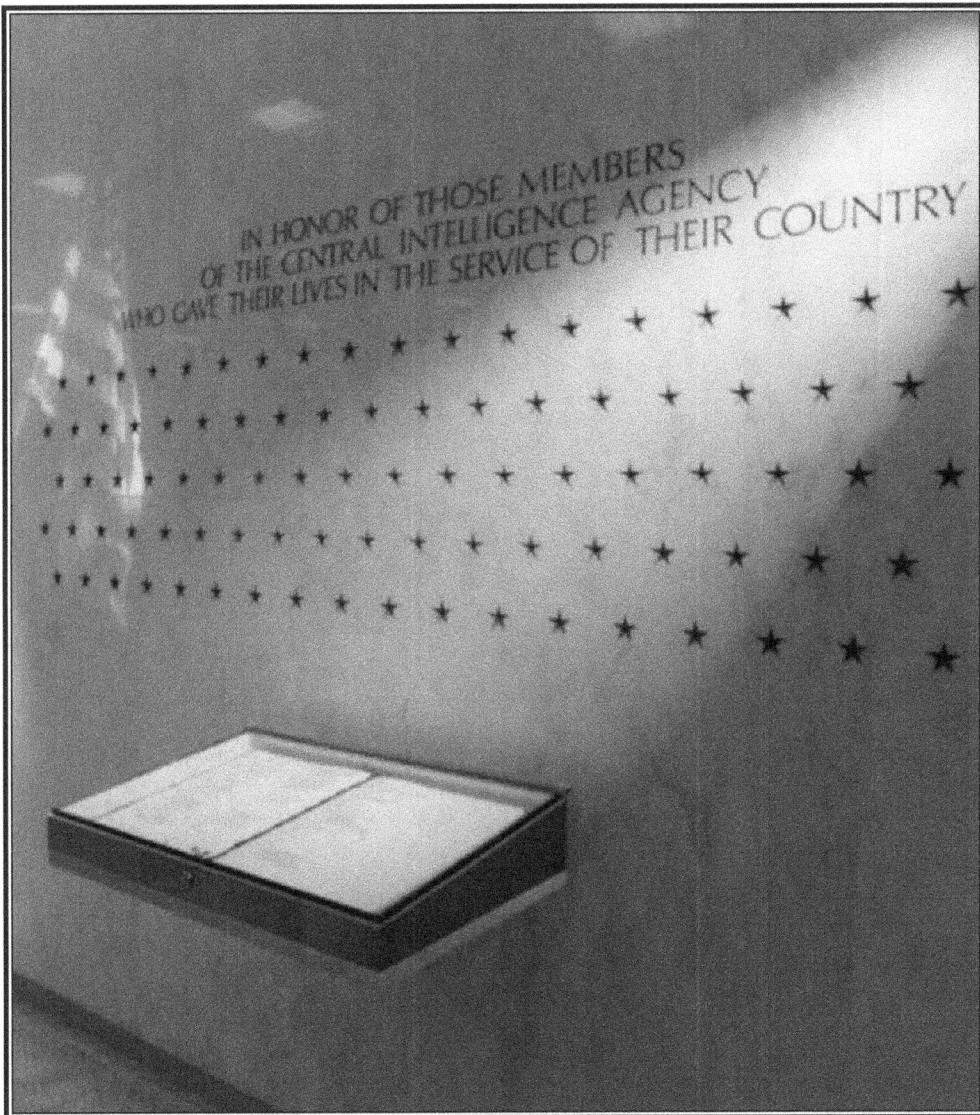

CIA Memorial Wall.

Contents

The Purpose

This anthology was prepared as a contribution to Department of Defense–led interagency efforts to commemorate the passing of 50 years since the large-scale engagement of the military forces of the United States and other countries in defending the Republic of Vietnam (South Vietnam) against communist guerrilla, mainforce, and North Vietnamese Army units. For CIA, and many members of the US military, engagement in South Vietnam began well before what is marked as the beginning of the 50th anniversary commemoration, 1965. As the 41 articles selected by CIA historian Clayton Laurie for this anthology will show, Southeast Asia was the focus of CIA activity as long ago as the early 1950s, when it was directed to provide support to French efforts to maintain control of its colony of Indochina.

Foreword

In his essay of introduction to the first-ever issue of *Studies in Intelligence* in 1955, "The Need for an Intelligence Literature," the founder of the nation's first journal on intelligence, Sherman Kent, wrote that the profession of intelligence had reached a high level of maturity and professionalism, but it lacked an essential ingredient of a true profession—a literature of its own. This was a "matter of great importance," he went on, and then explained why: "As long as this discipline lacks a literature, its method, its vocabulary, its body of doctrine, and even its fundamental theory run the risk of never reaching maturity." In the essay, he described the literature he thought was needed:

> *What I am talking about is a literature dedicated to the analysis of our many-sided calling, and produced by its most knowledgeable devotees . . . You might call it the institutional mind and memory of our discipline . . .*
>
> *The most important service that such a literature performs is the permanent recording of our new ideas and experiences. When we record, we not only make possible easier and wider communication of thought, we also take a rudimentary step towards making our findings cumulative.*

It is in this spirit that *Studies in Intelligence* offers this anthology of articles published on the conflict in Southeast Asia. This collection is also offered as a CIA contribution to the Defense Department–led effort to commemorate the passing of 50 years since the United States carried out its military commitment to the defense of the government of the Republic of Vietnam beginning in 1965 and ending in 1975. The 10-year-long commemoration is intended to provide opportunities to honor and thank the men and women engaged in the US defense of South Vietnam, both in military and nonmilitary functions.

For many—myself among them—who served in uniform in Vietnam and who walked the edges of rice paddies awaiting the next ambush or boobytrap, disembarked from helicopters under fire, clawed up mountainsides in the gunsights of Viet Cong or North Vietnamese troops, or manned outposts under constant artillery fire, intelligence was a mystery, little more than the occasional source of warnings that usually led to a sudden helicopter flight to some unexplored place or to an order to dig deeper holes and sharpen our vigilance. On occasion, when a prisoner was taken or some official-looking papers were found, orders were given to send them "back to intelligence," wherever that was. For the foot soldier, that was usually the end of it. But, of course, there was so much more to it than that—as I have come to learn in more than 40 years in the intelligence profession. And how different are today's intelligence-driven conflicts in which soldiers, sailors, airmen, and Marines know so much more about the intelligence that drives their operations?

We hope the articles in this collection will, for veterans of the conflict, lessen the mystery of national intelligence and serve to show them and students of the war the ways in which CIA at home attempted to honestly provide sound intelligence analysis to decisionmakers while, at the same time on Southeast Asian soil, it carried out operations aimed at contributing to the US military war effort.

The Center for the Study of Intelligence and the Editorial Board of *Studies in Intelligence* also hope this collection will serve as acknowledgment and tribute to the many people of the US intelligence and diplomatic communities and US and Allied armed forces who worked mightily and faithfully, too often sacrificing life and limb, in the pursuit of US goals in Southeast Asia.

Andres Vaart

Managing Editor
Studies in Intelligence

August 2016

Late in 1967, shortly before I resigned as the special assistant for Vietnam to Dr. R. J. Smith, CIA's deputy director for intelligence (DDI), I went to DCI Richard Helms to protest the publication over his signature of a national intelligence estimate in which the Defense Department's intelligence analysts had cut by half CIA's estimate of the size of the forces facing our troops in Vietnam. Mr. Helms's response was "Dick, the war is the Pentagon's show, and it's not our job to challenge their running of it."

Smith was DDI during much of the Vietnam War. Early in my tenure as his special assistant for Vietnam, he declared that the conflict was an "intelligence sideshow." The main enemy, the existential threat to America and the whole Western world, he reminded me, was our Cold War against the nuclear-armed Soviet Union, its occupation of Eastern Europe, and its avowed aim to subvert and supplant the world's established and budding democracies, and that was where our intelligence efforts had to be focused.

This anthology of *Studies in Intelligence* articles relating to the Vietnam conflict both reflects and challenges the perceptions held by Helms and Smith and, by his own admission, Secretary of Defense Robert McNamara. Over a period of years a relatively small number of DI analysts produced an impressive body of cogent, mostly pessimistic analyses of the military, economic, political, and psychological situation in Vietnam and the prospects for US success in thwarting what was perceived by American political leaders as the Communist Bloc's goal of overwhelming all of Southeast Asia. These products were exemplified in the so-called Pentagon Papers—which was largely a compilation of highly classified CIA intelligence analyses

Foreword

commissioned by McNamara and supervised by Smith—and in such *Studies in Intelligence* features as the dueling reviews of a book on the beginnings of America's involvement with Vietnam.

Similarly, a substantial, but still a small number of CIA operations and logistics officers relative to the size of their parent Directorates of Operations and Administration, devised and executed rural counterinsurgency programs that for a time and in limited areas beat back communist political-military infiltration of southern Indochina. In the peak years of the conflict, CIA's Saigon Station was the Agency's largest, fielding specialists from all four directorates who directly supported and often spearheaded embassy and Military Assistance Command, Vietnam (MACV) programs.

The 42 *Studies* articles in this collection touch on all of the above themes, both as they were considered during the conflict and on reflection years after the 1973 Paris Peace Accords essentially ended US involvement in the Vietnamese civil war. Among the articles that addressed topics as the conflict unfolded are the earliest four works in this anthology. Originally classified and appearing during 1962–65, they addressed from different points of view the intelligence aspects of the counterinsurgency strategy the John F. Kennedy administration had adopted for use in Southeast Asia. Each was written by a seasoned intelligence practitioner, and each reflected considerations that remain valid 50 years later. Other contemporaneous articles addressed more specific intelligence techniques in the war's context, including imagery analysis, battle damage assessment, targeting, assessment of HUMINT targets, and the estimative process that itself shaped US engagement in the region.

The January 1973 signing of the Paris Peace Accords led to US military disengagement, but it ushered in a period of remembrance and reflection that continues to this day. The readers of this anthology will see clearly that, "sideshow" or not, for CIA and US intelligence at large, the conduct of intelligence during the conflicts in Southeast Asia served as archetypal models of the complex contours of intelligence in the times of war that would regrettably follow.

Richard Kovar

Former Special Assistant for Vietnam to the DDI
and former Managing Editor of *Studies in Intelligence*

August 2016

時局圖

一目了然　　不言而喻

The conflicts in Southeast Asia during the period 1945–75 in some respects marked the conclusion of Asian nationalist efforts to recover sovereignty over their lands, which had been conquered and governed or dominated by foreign powers since the 19th century. This turn-of-the-century (1900) Chinese-produced map depicts the common, unkind characterizations many Asians held of the occupying powers, including the French, who governed Indochina. The caption around the map reads as follows: top—"map of the current situation"; left—"understand at a glance"; right: "no words need be spoken." Source: Wikicommons Maps.

Preface

The Contents

The works in this anthology are essentially arranged chronologically through the several phases of CIA engagement in the region. The first part of this anthology contains brief historical surveys written by Dr. Laurie of each of the phases to provide context for the selections identified after each section. The titles in these sections are hyperlinked to summaries of their contents, which are contained in the second part of the anthology. These, in turn, are hyperlinked to the locations of digital versions of the articles on the Internet.

The collection begins with the first decade after WWII and the end of the French colonial occupation of Indochina. This is followed by four sections covering US intelligence analysis and engagement from 1954 to the evacuation of 1975. The anthology closes with a section of essays that represent postwar reflections on the Southeast Asian experience.

Other Resources

Studies in Intelligence is housed in CIA's Center for the Study of Intelligence, which is also home to CIA's staff and contract historians. Throughout this anthology readers will find allusions to unclassified or declassified histories on the subjects of this anthology. Among these is the collection of histories written by Thomas L. Ahern, Jr. In addition, providing rich reference material is a National Intelligence Council–produced collection of some 170 intelligence estimates on the region, from the first estimate on the subject by the one-year-old CIA in 1948 to the last, "Assessment of the Situation in South Vietnam," published in March 1975. Hyperlinks to the online versions of these much longer works are provided throughout the digital form of this document. Yet another resource is the recently released collection of *President's Daily Briefs* produced during the administrations of Presidents John F. Kennedy and Lyndon B. Johnson.

Disclaimer. All statements of fact, opinion, or analysis expressed in the articles contained in this anthology are those of the authors. Nothing in them should be construed as asserting or implying US government endorsement of the factual statements or interpretations contained in them. *Studies in Intelligence* often includes copyright-protected material and permission should be sought before reprinting material contained herein.

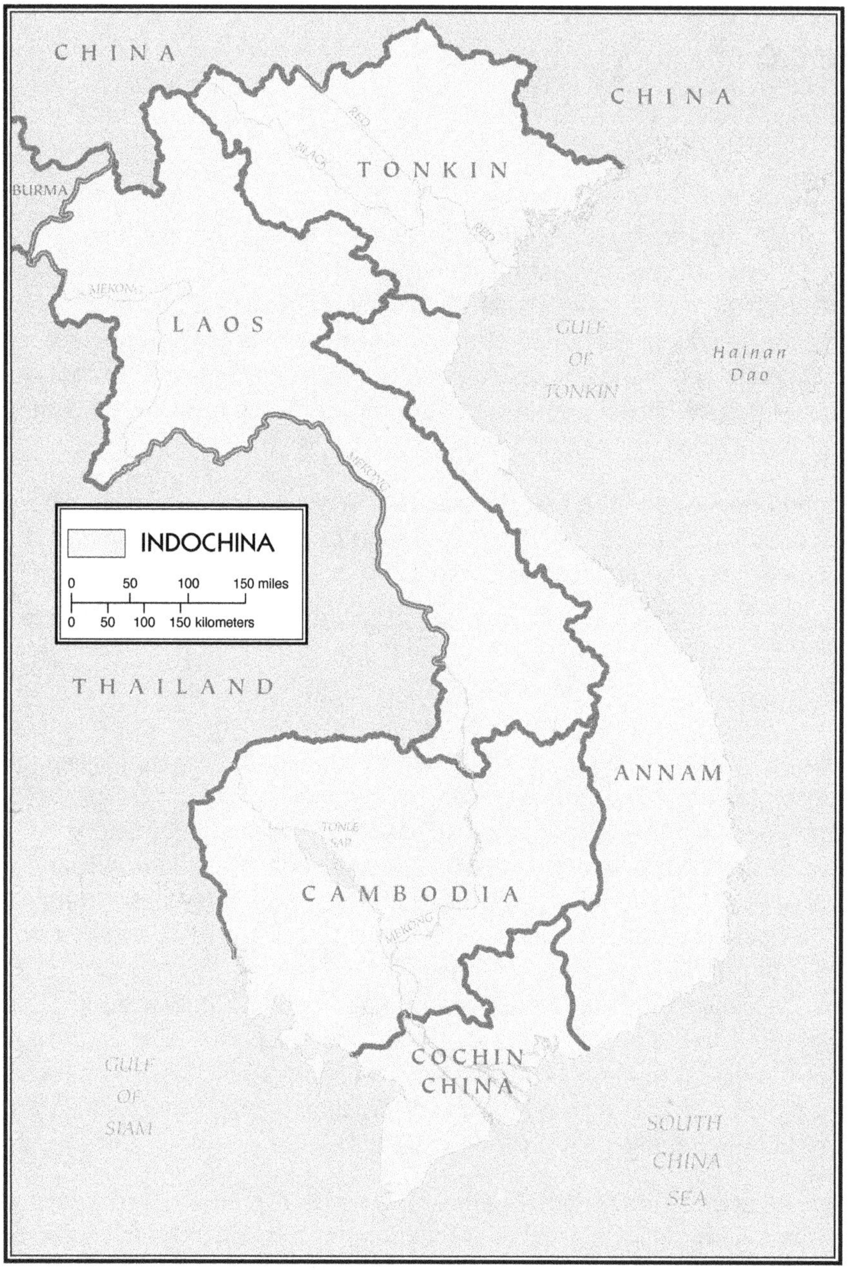
CHINA
CHINA
BURMA
TONKIN
LAOS
GULF OF TONKIN
Hainan Dao
INDOCHINA
0 50 100 150 miles
0 50 100 150 kilometers
THAILAND
ANNAM
CAMBODIA
COCHIN CHINA
GULF OF SIAM
SOUTH CHINA SEA
MEKONG
RED
BLACK
TONLE SAP

MPG 16-7607 6-16

The French governed Indochina until 1953. Laos and Cambodia gained independence in November 1953.

Indochina-In Support of a Colonial Power, 1945-54

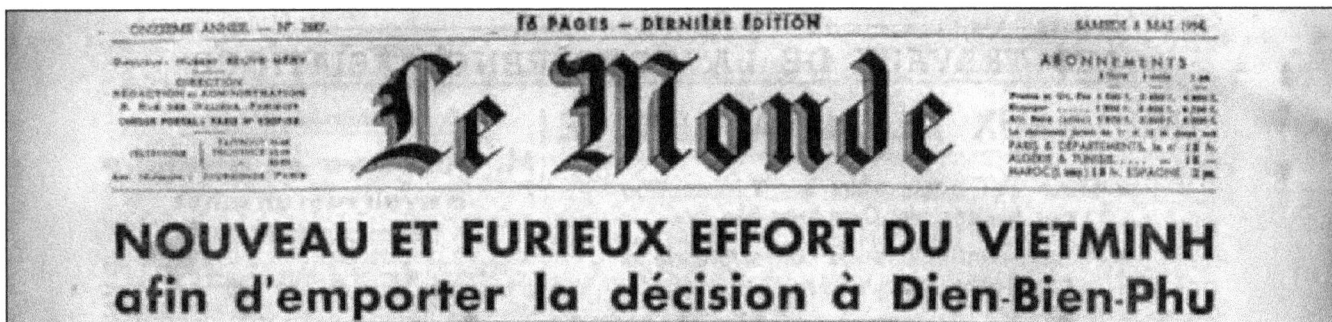

NOUVEAU ET FURIEUX EFFORT DU VIETMINH afin d'emporter la décision à Dien-Bien-Phu

The First US Foray into Indochina

The March 1965 arrival of US Marines on South Vietnam's northern beaches was not the first US foray into the region. As far back as 1944, units of the Office of Strategic Services (OSS), the Central Intelligence Agency's predecessor organization, were in contact with Vietnamese guerrilla groups operating in Tonkin, then part of the larger French colony of Indochina, which comprised Vietnam, Cambodia, and Laos. In 1945, an OSS team appeared from bases in Kunming, China, to collect intelligence on Japanese military strength and movements and to set up escape and evasion routes for downed Allied pilots.

Members of this group, known as the Deer Team, encountered members of a Vietnamese resistance organization known as the Viet Minh (League for the Independence of Vietnam). Ho Chi Minh and Vo Nguyen Giap established the group in May 1941 just after Japan had occupied Indochina—seven months before the attack on Pearl Harbor brought the United States into World War II. By 1945, the Viet Minh had set up a broad-based anti-Japanese guerrilla group consisting of nationalist noncommunist and communist Vietnamese who concurrently opposed French occupation of the region. The OSS team met with Ho and, determining that the Viet Minh were well motivated and organized, began to provide training and arms to support their resistance to the Japanese and to collect intelligence during the summer of 1945.

World War II's Aftermath

When Japan surrendered to the Allies in August 1945, Imperial forces in Indochina laid down their arms, leaving a power vacuum in the country. On 15 August, the Viet Minh, by then a large armed presence throughout Vietnam, seized a good portion of the country. OSS members accompanied Ho into Hanoi, where on 2 September 1945 he declared Vietnam's independence from France. Maj. Archimedes Patti of the Deer Team stood on the stage next to Ho during the address and listened to Ho quote passages from the US Declaration of Independence, which Patti had given him some time before. Three weeks later, on 26 September 1945, the first American serviceman died in Vietnam—OSS Maj. Albert Peter Dewey (USA), shot and killed at a Viet Minh roadblock in Saigon, a victim of mistaken identity.

When the Deer Team left Vietnam in October 1945 with the demobilization of the OSS, Patti and others sent reports to Washington encouraging a constructive relationship with Ho and the new Vietnamese government. President Franklin D. Roosevelt, like most Americans, was a steadfast anti-imperialist and believed European colonization of Asia was a root cause of World War II. Roosevelt also was a Francophobe and disliked French leader Charles de Gaulle. He thought the French had always been poor colonial administrators and were now a spent force in world affairs.

Header photo: The banner headline of the French newspaper Le Monde *of 8 May 1954 proclaimed, "The Vietminh open new and furious effort to reach a decision in Dien Bien Phu."*

Indochina–In Support of a Colonial Power, 1945–54

Patti's advice would have received a sympathetic hearing in the White House had Roosevelt still been living. FDR had opposed a French return to Indochina, instead pressing the idea of a United Nations trusteeship until an indigenous government, presumably representative of the people, could take over. Naturally, de Gaulle flatly rejected the idea. British Prime Minister Winston S. Churchill similarly opposed Roosevelt's plan, viewing UN trusteeships and the dissolution of the French empire as prelude toward a parallel dismantling of the much larger British Empire.

In the weeks after Roosevelt's death on 12 April 1945, the French had made it known to the new president, Harry S. Truman, that they would neither support US policies in postwar Europe nor support the United States in its dealings with an increasingly aggressive and bellicose Soviet Union unless Washington supported a French return to Indochina. The United States determined that concerns about Europe outweighed those of other areas of the world, and the Truman administration acquiesced and then actively supported French efforts to reestablish colonial rule in Indochina.

The First Indochina War Begins

The French incited the First Indochina War by forcefully reoccupying northern Vietnam in the fall of 1946, driving the Viet Minh from the cities into the countryside. The early years of this war consisted of a low-intensity guerrilla conflict throughout Indochina, though primarily in heavily populated areas of Vietnam and especially in Tonkin in the north. Within five years, many in France and the United States eventually came to see the continuing colonial war in Indochina as just another part of the global Cold War pitting the West, and especially the United States, against the Soviet Union.

US leaders generally accepted the validity of the "Domino Theory"—that held that if one nation in a region fell to communism, then its neighbors would inevitably fall, one "domino" after another. US officials thus came to see the insurgency in Vietnam as a communist-inspired first domino in Southeast Asia. US leaders also tended to see the existence of a monolithic communism in which communists everywhere operated in lockstep with dictates and vast conspiratorial plans for world conquest emanating from Moscow. Thus, the Truman and

Eisenhower administrations believed that a pro-Western Vietnam was crucial to the containment of communism, especially any southward expansion of the influence of the People's Republic of China, which had been established under Mao Zedong in October 1949.

US Funding and Presence in the French Indochina War

As a result, in 1950 the United States began to provide funding for the French military effort against the Viet Minh. Washington also formally recognized the French-sponsored Vietnamese government of Emperor Bao Dai. By 1953, the United States was funding roughly 80 percent of the cost of the Indochina War, employing the French as a proxy and bulwark against communism in Southeast Asia.

CIA placed its first intelligence operatives in Saigon and Hanoi in 1950, soon after the Truman administration officially recognized the Bao Dai government. These operatives soon reported to Washington that Ho was a populist hero with widespread support in both North and South Vietnam. Moreover, even with US equipment and money, the French were losing.

The French adopted a static military strategy in Vietnam, building a series of pillboxes, bunkers, and fortified strongpoints throughout the most populated areas of the north. Half a dozen French or French colonial troops occupied each location, but none would venture from their defenses. The US Military Assistance and Advisory Group, Indochina (MAAG), which had been established in 1950, unsuccessfully warned against use of this military strategy. Although the French experienced some brief success in 1951, they had lost control of the war by 1954—at that point French forces in Indochina had suffered more than 140,000 casualties, more than half of whom had been killed. Public support at home for what the French public had begun to call "The Dirty War" (Le Sale Guerre) declined sharply before the final significant French defeat between March and May 1954 at Dien Bien Phu in western Tonkin on the Laotian border. There, Giap's army surrounded and annihilated a sizeable French force.

Indochina–In Support of a Colonial Power, 1945–54

The Geneva Settlement of 1954

As that battle raged, US, French, British, Soviet, and Chinese delegations met in Geneva, Switzerland, to discuss Cold War issues, including those associated with the recently concluded Korean War and the fate of Indochina. When Dien Bien Phu fell, the French resolved to leave Indochina. By the terms of the international agreement reached in Geneva, Ho and the communists were to control Vietnam north of the 17th Parallel. Laos and Cambodia became neutral monarchies, and Emperor Bao Dai and his prime minister, Ngo Dinh Diem, were to administer the state of Vietnam below the 17th Parallel until elections in July 1956 decided on the leadership of a unified Vietnam. Neither the United States nor the South Vietnamese signed the final agreement.

In the wake of the Geneva settlement, then DCI Allen Dulles told Eisenhower's National Security Council that victory in the battle of Dien Bien Phu had tremendously boosted Ho's popularity. If elections took place as planned in July 1956, Ho would easily win and bring all of Vietnam under communist control. Dulles later recalled that the most "disheartening feature of the news from Indochina in the summer of 1954 was the evidence that a majority of the people in Vietnam supported the Viet Minh rebels."

Studies Selections:

LePage, Jean-Marc and Elie Tenenbaum. "French and American Intelligence Relations during the First Indochina War, 1950–1954." *Studies in Intelligence* 55, no. 3 (2011): 19–27. Originally UNCLASSIFIED.

Swift, Carleton A., Richard D. Kovar, and Russell J. Bowen. "Intelligence in Recent Public Literature: *Why Vietnam? Prelude to America's Albatross.*" *Studies in Intelligence* 25, no. 2 (1981): 99–116. Originally UNCLASSIFIED.

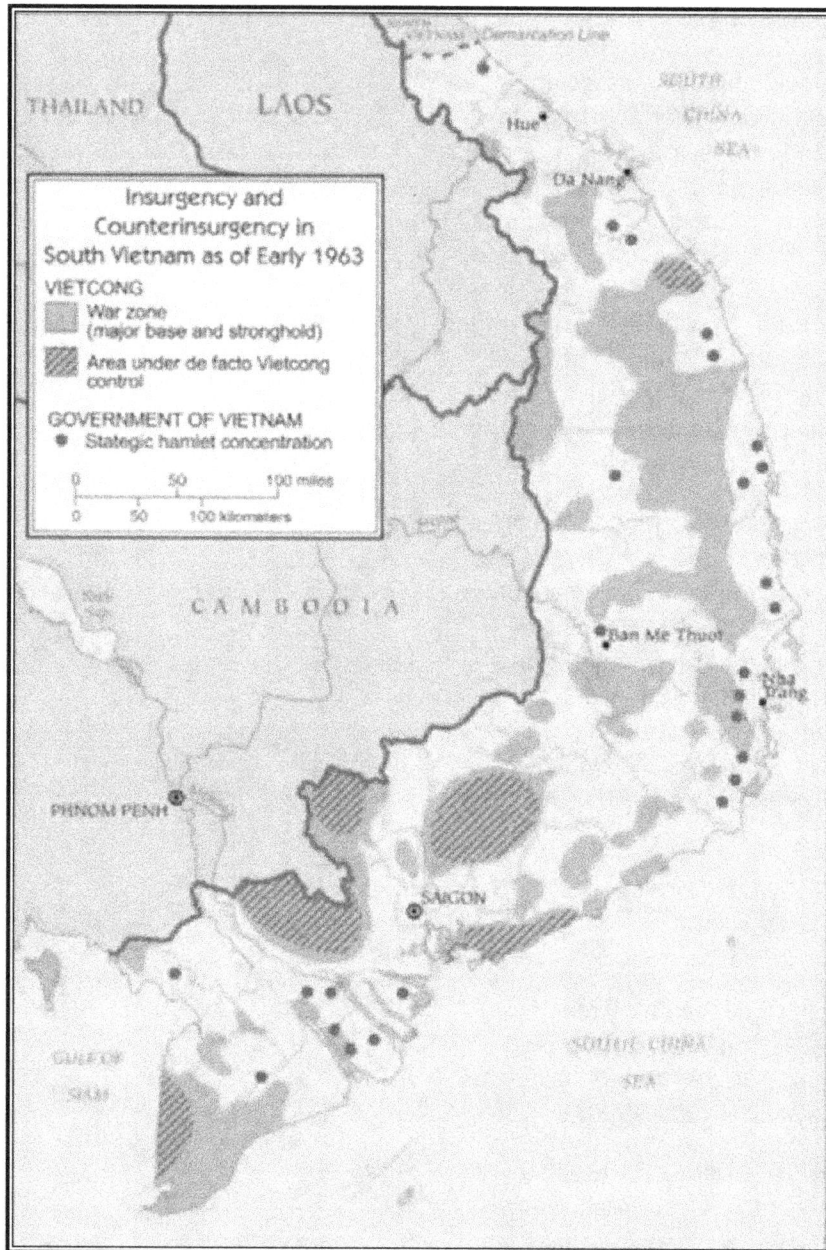

Insurgency and
Counterinsurgency in
South Vietnam as of Early 1963
VIETCONG
War zone
(major base and stronghold)
Area under de facto Vietcong
control
GOVERNMENT OF VIETNAM
● Stategic hamlet concentration
0   50   100 miles
0   50   100 kilometers

MPG 752085AI (C00033) 2-00

Map from Thomas L. Ahern, Jr., CIA and Rural Pacification in South
Vietnam *(Center for the Study of Intelligence, 2001). Originally classified,
the book was declassified in 2009. See cia.gov, FOIA Electronic Reading
Room, Vietnam Histories.*

The Republic of Vietnam, Insurgency and Nation-Building, 1954-65

US Advisers Arrive in South Vietnam

In an effort to reduce Ho's popularity and maintain a friendly, noncommunist Vietnamese government, the Eisenhower administration began to bolster the regime in the south. On 26 June 1954, CIA established the Saigon Military Mission under Air Force Col. Edward Lansdale. Lansdale operated from the US Embassy in Saigon as an air attaché and was charged with shoring up the Bao Dai/Diem regime. At the same time, the United States vastly increased its military support to South Vietnam to include the dispatch of some 300 military advisers.

Lansdale developed a close friendship with Diem. From 1954 until late 1956, he helped the prime minister survive several coups d'état by bribing opposition leaders and rigging an election in 1955 that ousted Bao Dai and established the Republic of Vietnam under Diem. Lansdale tried to convince Diem to become a "man of the people" and to reach out to the peasantry, something Diem disliked doing. Lansdale also advised him to create civic action programs, improve the rural infrastructure and educational system, and undertake land reform and a host of other programs to gain popular support—to win peasant "hearts and minds." Initially the United States viewed Diem, in President Eisenhower's words, as "the miracle man of Asia," the leader who could turn everything around in South Vietnam.

Lansdale Operations in North Vietnam

At the same time, Lansdale orchestrated a series of psychological and covert operations in North Vietnam, believing that while the United States did all it could

to stabilize the South, it could also undermine Ho in the North. These operations included destroying government printing presses, encouraging emigration, recruiting "stay-behind" teams, burying weapons caches, attempting to close the port of Haiphong, contaminating petroleum supplies, and sabotaging rail and bus lines. A number of CIA-sponsored paramilitary groups infiltrated the North under the direction of CIA's Lucien Conein.

While these covert operations had mixed results, one effort in 1954 and 1955, a propaganda campaign known as Operation Exodus, ultimately convinced 1.25 million North Vietnamese Catholics to emigrate to the south. With the aid of the US Navy's 7th Fleet and CIA proprietary airlines, hordes of terror-stricken evacuees fled as news cameras captured dramatic footage that would be shown worldwide. The campaign's slogan, "God has Gone South," reverberated around the world and blackened Ho's hitherto untarnished public reputation in the world. When the evacuation ended, so did most of Lansdale's other covert operations. The Saigon Military Mission (and thus the CIA) closed its doors in December 1956. The 1956 election to determine the final government of a unified Vietnam had not been held.

Enter the Viet Cong and Viet Cong Infrastructure

By the late 1950s, the United States began to have doubts about the stubborn and uncooperative

---

Header photo: Special Forces team quarters in Civilian Irregular Defense Group Headquarters in Khe Sanh, Quang Tri Province, ca. 1963. CIA photo.

The Republic of Vietnam, Insurgency and Nation-Building, 1954–65

president of South Vietnam they supported. Diem's increasingly autocratic and dictatorial policies proved counterproductive to US aims, and, by 1959, he led an unpopular and repressive police state run by cronies and family members. Members of the Viet Minh, who had remained in the South and continued to be loyal to Ho and the communist regime in the North, became the prime targets of the Diem regime. They responded by beginning a guerrilla campaign to topple Diem's government. This indigenous opposition, which Diem in 1956 branded the Viet Cong (VC—a contraction for Vietnamese Communists), received increasing aid from the North, primarily in the form of political and military cadres and arms, although not yet North Vietnamese troops.

The VC drew its members from the South Vietnamese population and formed one of several forces that the US military and CIA faced. One group of VC, divided into local, district, and provincial irregular forces, was composed of peasants dressed in traditional black pajama-style clothing and sandals made of old tires who worked in the fields by day and took up arms at night. After 1961, another Viet Cong group, called the People's Liberation Front, created main force units consisting of organized conventional units with formalized command structures and uniforms.

Complementing and assisting these military forces was the Viet Cong Infrastructure (VCI), a virtual government paralleling Saigon's. It was composed of political commissars, military recruiters, tax collectors, and functionaries operating throughout South Vietnam's villages. Competing with the Saigon government for influence, by 1965 the VCI maintained a near full-time presence in upwards of 80 percent of the villages and hamlets of the south. Until the VCI's arrival, some areas, such as the heavily populated Binh Dinh Province on the coast, had never been under government control after 1945. The VCI became a primary CIA target in the late 1960s.

CIA Returns to Lead Irregular Groups

After a five-year hiatus, CIA returned to Vietnam in 1961, when 93 operations officers arrived to establish the Civilian Irregular Defense Groups, or CIDG. The CIDG was the idea of Gilbert Layton and David Nuttle,

who believed that defending the civilian population from the Viet Cong through village-based programs could defeat the communists. They drew on the experiences of those who had served with the Saigon Military Mission. With the help of hundreds of US Army Special Forces soldiers, part of the recently created Green Berets who supplemented the CIA effort with much-needed firepower and logistics, the program combined self-defense training with social and economic initiatives to gain the allegiance of the rural highlands people.

CIA determined that rural peasants, a relatively immobile population composed of tight-knit social groups, had thorough knowledge of local terrain and were willing to defend their villages against Viet Cong intimidation or attacks. Civic action programs such as these were an integral part of the CIDG's mission, which sought to improve the standard of living for the rural population while rolling back VCI gains. CIA created several CIDG teams in the central highlands of South Vietnam.

CIA's officers began by first using the Montagnard hill people as a test group. The Montagnards lived in relatively isolated areas and received no protection or services from the South Vietnamese government. Trained and equipped by CIA and assisted by Green Berets, the CIDG militias did very well in combat against Viet Cong forces in their local areas. Due to overwhelming CIDG successes in 1962 and 1963, the South Vietnamese government could declare the central highlands province of Darlac entirely clear of communist influence. By mid-1963, the CIDG operated 27 camps, controlling 40,000 militia and 11,000 strike force troops. They succeeded in securing several hundred villages, inhabited by some 300,000 civilians, over an area of several hundred square miles.

SWITCHBACK: CIA Loses CIDG

As the CIDG program appeared to be succeeding in 1962, CIA leaders requested additional Special Forces personnel to expand operations into the more heavily populated lowland areas of the South. The request caught the attention of US military leaders, who were in the process of expanding the US military role in South Vietnam. Although CIA was using only some 400 Special Forces personnel at the time of its request, the newly created Military Assistance Command, Vietnam (MACV)

The Republic of Vietnam, Insurgency and Nation-Building, 1954–65

held that the Green Beret mission should emphasize offensive combat operations and not static pacification or peasant militia programs. Army leaders believed that the CIDG program represented a CIA-directed misuse of the Special Forces. In addition, military leaders pointed out that the CIA role in CIDG had expanded beyond its original mission to carry out small covert actions.

In part, this perspective was a product of the Bay of Pigs debacle in Cuba in early 1961, after which the John F. Kennedy administration concluded that CIA could not effectively run large paramilitary operations. As a result, in 1963 the administration endorsed transfer—Operation SWITCHBACK—of the CIDG program from CIA to MACV. This effectively ended CIA participation in paramilitary programs of its own creation for several years to come.

Thereafter, CIA provided only advice, assistance, and intelligence to MACV programs. The Special Forces took over the CIDG program and entirely changed its scope. What had been a set of village defense units responsible for localized rural security became mercenary long-range reconnaissance and patrol units that redeployed to the Laotian and Cambodian borders.

Strategic Hamlet Program

In addition to the CIDG program, and in cooperation with the Saigon government, CIA helped launch in February 1962 another ambitious village-level counterinsurgency effort. Ngo Dinh Nhu, President Diem's brother, directed the initiative, which included the Strategic Hamlet Program. Like an earlier effort known as the Agroville Program (1959–61), the Strategic Hamlet Program aimed to move peasants from areas of Viet Cong influence into fortified village compounds. There, land redistribution and social programs presumably would win the allegiance of the populace. By the end of 1962, more than 2,600 hamlets had been relocated and fortified. The program had critical flaws, however. First, it proved difficult, if not impossible, to identify and separate Viet Cong members among the South Vietnamese peasants. The Strategic Hamlets themselves also proved easy targets. The entire program remained underfunded, understaffed, and underdefended. Eventually, it came to epitomize the corruption, inefficiency, and repressive nature of the Diem regime and created resentment among displaced peasants.

The Downfall of the Diem Regime

The Kennedy administration found stabilization efforts increasingly difficult. Diem's continuing repressive policies proved ever more counterproductive, especially in the summer of 1963 when South Vietnamese troops acting on Diem's orders ruthlessly put down nationwide antigovernment Buddhist demonstrations. This action blatantly contradicted promises Diem had made to President Kennedy.

Although the US government officially continued to support a democratic South Vietnam, several individuals in the US State Department and the National Security Council wanted to get rid of Diem's regime with a replacement more amenable to US advice. Then DCI John McCone, among others, opposed a coup, however. He predicted that a series of revolving-door governments worse than Diem's would result and hinder further gains or destroy what had been achieved to date.

McCone also predicted a coup would result in deterioration of the military situation. He later recalled that he had told President Kennedy in the fall of 1963, "Mr. President, if I was manager of a baseball team, [and] I had only one pitcher, I would keep him on the mound whether he was a good pitcher or not." McCone did not instruct CIA personnel to support, hinder, or in any way prevent officers in the Army of the Republic of Vietnam (ARVN) from staging a coup. Nearly 15 years of US military, diplomatic, and financial aid had failed to create a stable government in South Vietnam.

Through the summer and fall of 1963, a cabal of ARVN generals plotted to topple Diem. CIA's Lucien Conein served as a covert liaison between the US ambassador to South Vietnam, Henry Cabot Lodge, Jr., and the senior officers plotting the coup, and while he had no responsibility for assisting or advising the plotters, he appears to have informed US officials in-country of an imminent revolt.

The coup against Diem started on the morning of 1 November 1963. Although Diem and his brother escaped from the presidential palace in Saigon that day, they later agreed to turn themselves over to the rebellious generals for safe passage out of the country. Instead, an ARVN officer shot and killed both men in the back of an

The Republic of Vietnam, Insurgency and Nation-Building, 1954–65

armored personnel carrier. The killings came as a shock to US leaders, especially President Kennedy, who never wanted a coup to end in that way.

The Johnson Administration Faces Larger War

As McCone had predicted, after Diem's death the Republic of Vietnam endured a succession of short-lived juntas for nearly two years. Fourteen governments, comprising ARVN generals and civilians, unsuccessfully attempted to create political stability and mount an effective military response to the Viet Cong, who, with growing assistance from North Vietnamese cadres, expanded control over more areas of South Vietnam.

Nearly 15 years of US military, diplomatic, and financial aid beginning in 1950 had failed to have any significant impact on creation of a stable government in South Vietnam. This situation frustrated those in the administration of Lyndon B. Johnson who had become president on 22 November 1963 after John F. Kennedy's assassination in Dallas, Texas.

In early 1964, President Johnson asked DCI McCone for CIA's assessment of the Vietnam situation, particularly why American efforts to date had produced no positive or lasting results. He also asked CIA analysts to assess what would happen to the rest of Southeast Asia if Laos and Vietnam came under North Vietnamese control. On 9 June 1964, CIA responded that,

. . . with the possible exception of Cambodia, it is unlikely that any nation in the area would quickly succumb to Communism as the result of the fall of Laos and South Vietnam. Furthermore, a continuation of Communism in the area would not be inexorable and any spread which did occur would take time—time in which the total situation may change in any number of ways unfavorable to the Communist cause.

The CIA analysis in 1964 conceded that the loss of Vietnam and Laos would profoundly damage the US position in the Far East and raise the prestige of China as a leader of world communism at the expense of the Soviet Union. Yet the CIA concluded that

. . . so long as the United States could retain its bases, such as those in Okinawa, Guam, the Philippines, and Japan, it would wield enough military power in Asia to deter China and North Vietnam from overt military aggression against Southeast Asia in general. Even in the worst-case scenario if Vietnam and Laos were to fall, the United States would still retain some leverage to affect the final outcome in Southeast Asia.

This analysis clearly refuted the Domino Theory accepted by the US government since the mid-1950s. In addition, CIA continued to send pessimistic reports that the insurgency in South Vietnam was growing even more threatening. The analysis had little impact on the Johnson administration. The president largely ignored the assessment and continued to treat South Vietnam as the first domino under attack by monolithic world communism under Ho Chi Minh, a communist puppet of the Kremlin.

Indeed, by late 1964 evidence was mounting that fully equipped North Vietnamese regulars of the People's Army of Vietnam (PAVN) were entering South Vietnam in substantial numbers via a supply route—the Ho Chi Minh Trail—through Laos and Cambodia. Their presumed intent: to capitalize on South Vietnam's instability and overthrow the government before increased US military and financial aid arrived.

In Washington, notwithstanding the CIA estimate, these developments prompted a wholesale change of perspective. Until then, policymakers had viewed communist activities in South Vietnam as homegrown, with some outside support. The Johnson administration took the view that North Vietnam had initiated and continued to feed the conflict. With that decision, the United States would take aggressive steps against North Vietnam to convince the communist leadership in Hanoi to cease its campaign to take over the South.

Infiltration into the North

Johnson's response was to intensify pressure on North Vietnam through conventional military and clandestine means. In early 1964, MACV developed plans for a series of covert operations against the North. The Operations Plan, or OPLAN 34A, was a military-controlled repetition of CIA paramilitary and sabotage operations against the North that had already produced dismal results on a smaller scale.

The Republic of Vietnam, Insurgency and Nation-Building, 1954–65

The MACV initiatives also failed. In fact, one such operation precipitated the Gulf of Tonkin Incident when, in early August 1964, North Vietnamese gunboats attacked US Navy vessels. Before the attack, MACV, under OPLAN 34A had assisted South Vietnamese commando raids on radar installations on the southern coast of North Vietnam. Simultaneously, the US Navy was conducting electronic intelligence (ELINT) collection missions nearby in the South China Sea. The North Vietnamese, thinking these US Navy destroyers were part of the recent coastal raids, attacked the USS Maddox and later, contemporaries thought, the USS Turner Joy.

The Johnson administration viewed the North Vietnamese actions as a direct provocation and, according to contingency plans already in place under OPLAN 34A, launched reprisal airstrikes against targets in the North (known as Operation PIERCE ARROW) as a warning to Hanoi not to launch further attacks and to cease aiding the Viet Cong in the South. At the same time, President Johnson sought a resolution from Congress authorizing him to use military force to protect American lives from communist attacks in the region.

The CIA analysis of the Gulf of Tonkin incident maintained that the attacks on the US destroyers by the North Vietnamese were a defensive reaction motivated by the North Vietnamese belief that the ELINT vessels were supporting the South Vietnamese commando raids. CIA concluded that the communists did not intend their actions to appear as a direct provocation to the United States.

The reprisals did not prevent additional communist aggression targeting US military personnel in South Vietnam between late 1964 and early 1965, resulting in American deaths. By late 1964 and early 1965, CIA assessments stated that the Viet Cong—with the advantage of increased North Vietnamese aid—were stronger than ever and that South Vietnam was on the verge of defeat.

In response to increased Viet Cong provocations and growing strength, the Johnson administration initiated a graduated bombing program against North Vietnam known as Operation FLAMING DART. That was soon followed by a more intense and sustained bombing campaign known as Operation ROLLING THUNDER.

The administration believed these bombing campaigns would convince Hanoi that assistance to the Viet Cong would carry an increasing cost in damage to the North's fledgling industrial infrastructure and that the leadership in Hanoi would seek respite through a negotiated end to the conflict. ROLLING THUNDER took place between March 1965 and October 1968, with bombing runs by Navy aircraft-carrier-based air units on the Yankee Station in the South China Sea and by Air Force units based in South Vietnam.

Following the start of the bombing campaign, the Johnson administration committed the first large detachment of US Marines to Da Nang, South Vietnam, on 8 March 1965 to protect air bases there. In April 1965, General William C. Westmoreland, the MACV commander, warned that the situation in South Vietnam was dire. Acting on this, the Joint Chiefs of Staff committed US ground forces to prevent the imminent collapse of Vietnam, sending three US Army divisions to help stabilize the government and enable the South Vietnamese Army to defend the nation on their own.

On the same day in 1965 that the United States decided on a sizeable troop commitment to South Vietnam, CIA issued a special memorandum that emphasized the bleakness of the US position there. CIA analysts noted that Viet Cong strength stood at roughly 150,000 men and that, if the US committed large numbers of ground combat forces into South Vietnam, it ran the risk of Americans assuming an even greater share of the fighting.

Just before DCI McCone resigned in April 1965, in part due to policy differences with President Johnson over the escalation, he sent a letter to the president in which he stated that based on CIA operative reports, ROLLING THUNDER was not working as planned and would fail to achieve its intended goals. McCone warned President Johnson that the United States risked "an ever-increasing commitment of US personnel without materially improving the chances of victory . . . In effect, we will find ourselves mired down in combat in the jungle in a military effort that we cannot win, and from which we will have extreme difficulty in extracting ourselves."

The Republic of Vietnam, Insurgency and Nation-Building, 1954-65

Studies Selections:

Ahern, Thomas L. Jr. "The CIA and the Government of Ngo Dinh Diem." *Studies in Intelligence* 37, no. 4 (1993): 41–51. Originally SECRET—Released in part.

Allen, George W. "Covering Coups in Saigon." *Studies in Intelligence* 33, no. 4 (1989): 57–61. Originally SECRET—Released in part.

Hartness, William M. "Aspects of Counterinsurgency Intelligence." *Studies in Intelligence* 7, no. 4 (1963): 71–83. Originally CONFIDENTIAL—Released in full.

Matthias, Willard C. "How Three Estimates Went Wrong." *Studies in Intelligence* 12, no. 1 (1968): 27–38. Originally SECRET//NOFORN—Released in part.

Palmer, Gen. Bruce. "US Intelligence and Vietnam." *Studies in Intelligence* 28, no. 5 (Special Issue, 1984). Originally SECRET//NOFORN—Released in part.

Schiattareggia, M. H. "Counterintelligence in Counter-Guerrilla Operations." *Studies in Intelligence* 6, no. 3 (1962): 1–24. Originally SECRET—Released in full and reprinted in *Studies in Intelligence* 57, No. 2 (June 2013): 39–63.

Schwarzchild, Edward T. "The Assessment of Insurgency." *Studies in Intelligence* 7, no. 4 (1963): 85–89. Originally SECRET—Released in full.

Smith, Russell Jack. "Intelligence Production during the Helms Regime." *Studies in Intelligence* 39, no. 4 (1995): 93–102. Originally SECRET—Released in part.

Steinmeyer, Walter. "The Intelligence Role in Counterinsurgency." *Studies in Intelligence* 9, no. 4 (1965): 57–63. Originally SECRET—Released in full and reprinted in *Studies in Intelligence* 59, no. 4 (December 2015). Steinmeyer is a penname for a former senior operations officer, Theodore Shackley.

A US Air Force O-1 observation plane, shown here overflying South Vietnam. The aircraft was used throughout Southeast Asia to spot, target, and evaluate strikes on enemy forces. US Air Force photo.

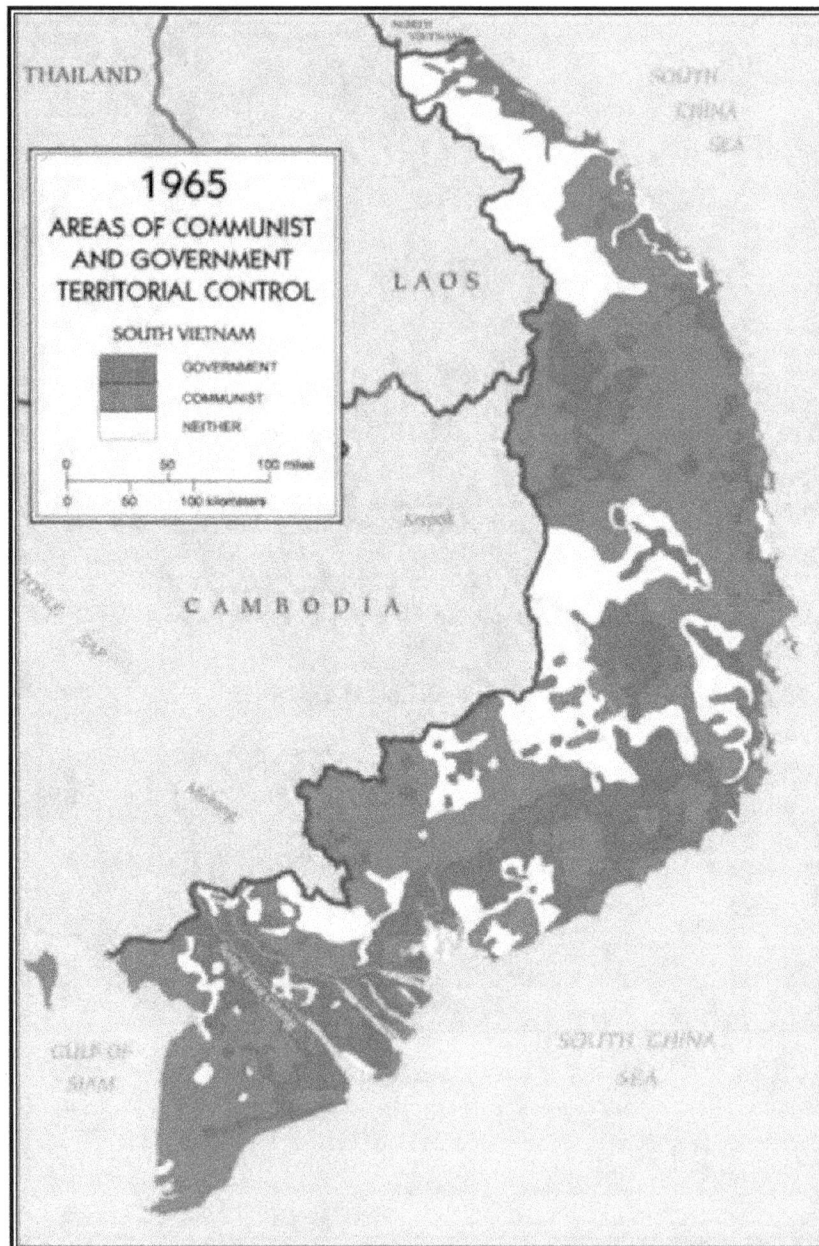

1965

AREAS OF COMMUNIST
AND GOVERNMENT
TERRITORIAL CONTROL

SOUTH VIETNAM

GOVERNMENT
COMMUNIST
NEITHER

0   50   100 miles
0   50   100 kilometers

MPG 752095AI (C00033) 2-00

Map from Thomas L. Ahern, Jr., CIA and Rural Pacification in South Vietnam (Center for the Study of Intelligence, 2001). Originally classified, the book was declassified in 2009. See cia.gov, FOIA Electronic Reading Room, Vietnam Histories.

The War "Goes Big," 1965–75

The "Other War" Against VCI Languishes

The United States fought a conventional—sometimes termed "Big Unit"—war in Vietnam during most of the second half of the 1960s and early 1970s. Between 1965 and 1973, more than 2 million US troops rotated into and out of Southeast Asia. Their number reached a peak in South Vietnam of approximately 570,000 in early 1969. During this period, both US and South Vietnamese forces paid only passing attention to rural pacification and village-level security, what many later termed "the other war" against the Viet Cong Infrastructure.

The CIA never regarded the conflict in Southeast Asia as its primary target for intelligence collection or analysis. Nor did it regard military support as its primary mission. Instead, CIA focused on the greater threats posed by the nuclear-armed Soviet Union and the People's Republic of China. Still, CIA reached a maximum commitment of some 500 personnel in-country in 1968.

As seen in the introduction to Part I, CIA waged a different sort of war from US conventional forces early on in Southeast Asia, focusing on rural security programs, which it continued to do as a conventional war went on around them. During this period, the US military adopted a nationwide "search-and-destroy" strategy, involving highly mobile helicopter-borne forces and intensive firepower. It was a war of attrition, with "body counts" serving as measures of success.

Meanwhile, the ROLLING THUNDER bombing campaign against North Vietnam initiated in 1965 and carried out through late 1968 never produced the desired results. The lack of a modern military-industrial infrastructure in the North meant that strategic bombing, like the kind used in World War II, had little impact on the communists' ability to wage war, their will to persist, or their ability to provide manpower and materiel support to the Viet Cong and the North Vietnamese forces fighting in the South. Intended as a political-diplomatic tool to induce the North to enter into negotiations, rather than as a potentially war-ending and devastating military weapon, ROLLING THUNDER achieved neither end.

"Escalating Stalemate"

As DCI John McCone had predicted, the responsibilities of the US military grew as the communists matched each US troop commitment in an "escalating stalemate," all while the South Vietnamese role diminished. CIA analysts had noted as early as 1965 that the South Vietnamese government and military were fraught with incompetence, factionalism, and corruption, which only aided the communists. Meanwhile, every pessimistic assessment of US foreign policy and real or implied criticism of the military delivered to the Oval Office further alienated the DCI and his agency from President Johnson, top policymakers in the Defense and State Departments, and military commanders and their intelligence staffs. The administration came to conclude that CIA was not a team player. John McCone left the CIA in early April 1965 convinced that the the administration would ultimately fail to achieve a stable, democratic, and friendly Republic of Vietnam.

Header photo: US Marines landing in South Vietnam on 8 March 1965. US Marine Corps photo.

The War "Goes Big," 1965-75

A New DCI and a "Vietnam Center" at CIA

McCone's replacement as DCI was a retired, highly decorated US naval officer with significant combat command experience, Vice Admiral William F. "Red" Raborn. Sworn in on 28 April 1965, Raborn would spend only 14 months as DCI. Although he would be much underrated in CIA history, Raborn's interaction with the president over Vietnam policies were considerably less fraught than those of McCone or Raborn's successor, Richard M. Helms.

One of DCI Raborn's most noteworthy innovations was the August 1965 creation in CIA of the office of the Special Assistant for Vietnam Affairs (SAVA), a "wild directorate" into which every officer, and only the "spark plugs"—the best Vietnam analysts the CIA could muster—would be placed. Led by a senior officer with the rank of deputy director, SAVA would provide the one and only voice briefing the DCI and the president on Vietnam-related matters. While Raborn's Deputy Director of Central Intelligence Richard Helms had initially shown little enthusiasm for the new office, he soon began to appreciate the advantages of the centralization of multitudinous and disparate offices fielding demands posed by Vietnam, especially in controlling a daily and massive flow of cables, dispatches, and memoranda. SAVA soon became CIA's clearinghouse for all Vietnam-related information from the four CIA directorates.

Richard Helms—The Third Vietnam-Era DCI-Takes Over

Richard Helms became DCI in 1966 at a time when White House meetings sounded like pep rallies for the war effort. Nevertheless, Helms felt that CIA "needed to stay at the table and keep the game honest." He viewed with great pride invitations to the president's exclusive "Tuesday Lunches," where Johnson discussed policy in an informal setting with those he considered his top advisers. Throughout, however, CIA continued to provide accurate, realistic assessments, no matter how unpopular or pessimistic they might have been. Like McCone, Helms remained skeptical about the chances of a US military victory in Vietnam. While a staunch CIA advocate at the White House, he often clashed with military leaders over issues such as the effectiveness of ROLLING THUNDER, the control of covert actions, the strength and nature of communist military forces, and the lack of attention to rural security and pacification.

The most important controversy of Helms's tenure involved contention over differing assessments of the size of communist units engaged in the South. Amid growing controversy over the war at home by 1967, the Johnson administration increased pressure on his military leaders to show progress. This they did by offering estimates that communist forces in South Vietnam had decreased significantly during two years of intensive combat action to some 270,000 fighters, largely North Vietnamese Army regulars.

CIA assessments, however, were starkly at odds with MACV's. CIA analysts estimated that 600,000 enemy fighters, including Viet Cong militias, Viet Cong Main Force units, and North Vietnamese regulars were actively engaged in South Vietnam. During a visit to the United States in late November 1967, General William Westmoreland, carrying the military's estimate, stated publicly and before Congress that the war would soon wind down. Basing his judgment on big losses North Vietnamese forces were suffering in large unit actions at the time, he predicted an imminent and successful conclusion, perhaps within a year.

CIA analysts countered that the military's focus on North Vietnamese units ignored or dismissed as unimportant large numbers of Viet Cong militia and main force fighters. To avoid a schism within the intelligence and defense communities, Helms overruled his embattled analysts and allowed the removal of the larger CIA numbers from key judgments of order-of-battle estimates, relegating them to the back pages and agreeing to accept the military's figures. President Johnson received a smaller, compromise count of 334,000 communist troops—larger than the MACV estimate but much smaller than CIA's.

The 1968 Tet Turning Point

The communist offensive that erupted during Tet, the Vietnamese New Year holiday, in late January 1968, demonstrated the accuracy of CIA estimates, as the very units that CIA analysts had warned about and which MACV had dismissed carried out attacks on US and South Vietnamese forces throughout South Vietnam.

The War "Goes Big," 1965–75

Major assaults took place on high-profile targets in large urban centers including Saigon, Da Nang, and the ancient capital Hue. The ability of communist forces to conduct a monthlong, nationwide campaign essentially verified CIA assessments of the fighting capability and potential impact of Viet Cong irregular forces and the Viet Cong Infrastructure on the war in the South. The controversy was eventually settled in July 1970, with CIA estimates gaining acceptance as official figures to be used for planning purposes.

The 1968 Tet offensive proved to be a turning point in the war. Although a communist military defeat, it was a psychological victory over the American public, which increasingly came to doubt Johnson administration pronouncements that the conflict would soon end in a US victory. In suggesting that the end of the conflict was nowhere in sight, the Tet offensive created a "credibility gap" between government statements about Vietnam and what appeared through news reports to actually be happening on the battlefields. It was a gap that would grow over time. Tet also revealed that the big-unit war waged since 1965 had not succeeded in inhibiting North Vietnamese efforts or in quelling the Viet Cong insurgency. If the communists retained the capability to launch a nationwide offensive like Tet, then American military and diplomatic policies needed to be reevaluated.

Studies Selections:

Atkins, Merle, Kenneth C. Fuller, and Bruce Smith. "'Rolling Thunder' and Bomb Damage to Bridges." *Studies in Intelligence* 13, no. 4 (1969): 1–9. Originally SECRET//NOFORN—Released in full.

Ford, Harold P. "The US Decision to Go Big in Vietnam." *Studies in Intelligence* 29, no. 1 (1985): 1–15. Originally SECRET//NOFORN—Released in full.

Hall, Arthur B. "Landscape Analysis." *Studies in Intelligence* 11, no. 3 (1967): 65–75. Originally SECRET//NOFORN—Released in full.

Kitchens, Allen H. "Crisis and Intelligence: Two Case Studies [Tet and Iran]." *Studies in Intelligence* 28, no. 3 (1984): 71–78. Originally UNCLASSIFIED.

Puchalla, Edward F. "Communist Defense Against Aerial Surveillance in Southeast Asia." *Studies in Intelligence* 14, no. 2 (1970): 31–78. Originally SECRET//NOFORN—Released in full.

Sinclair, Robert, "One Intelligence Analyst Remembers Another: A Review of *Who the Hell Are We Fighting? The Story of Sam Adams and the Vietnam Intelligence Wars.*" *Studies in Intelligence* 50, No. 4 (2006): 1–9. Originally UNCLASSIFIED.

Tidwell, William A. "A New Kind of Air Targeting." *Studies in Intelligence* 11, no. 1 (1967): 55–60. Originally CONFIDENTIAL//NOFORN—Released in full.

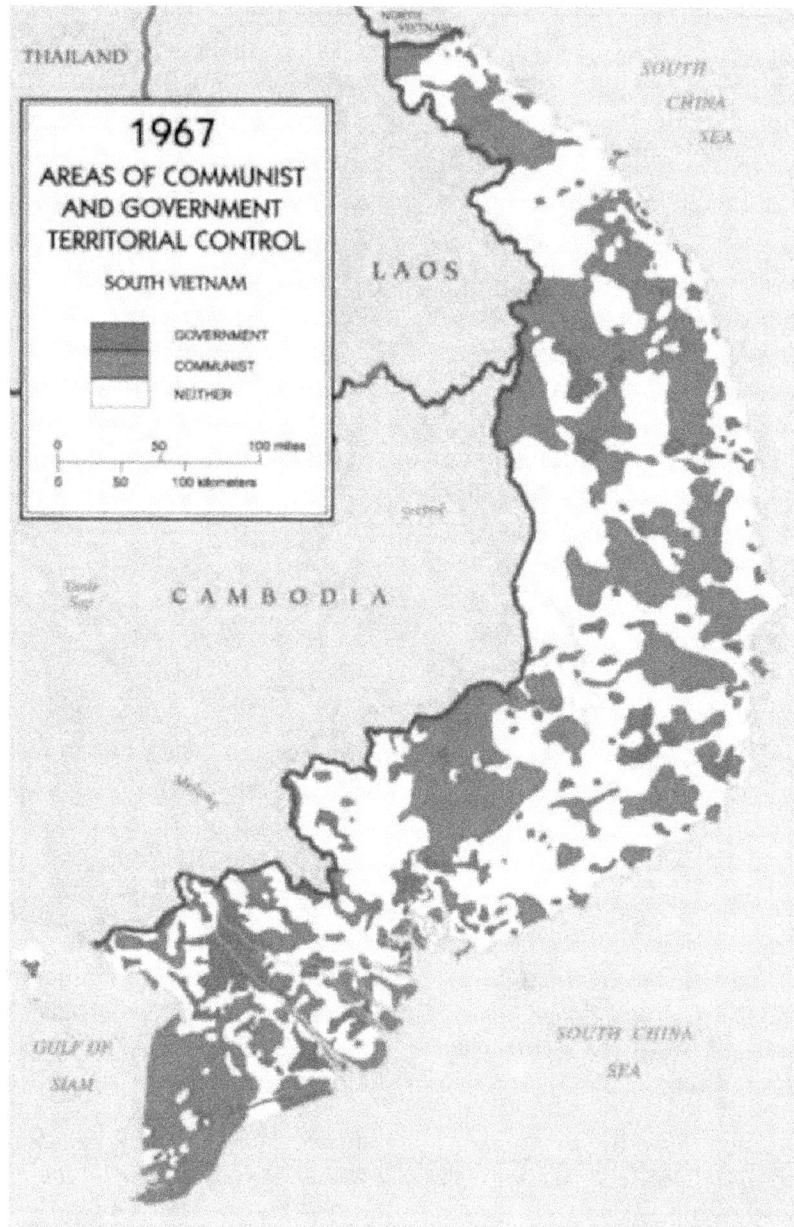

1967

AREAS OF COMMUNIST AND GOVERNMENT TERRITORIAL CONTROL

SOUTH VIETNAM

GOVERNMENT
COMMUNIST
NEITHER

MPG 752096AI (C00033) 2-00

Map from Thomas L. Ahern, Jr., CIA and Rural Pacification in South Vietnam *(Center for the Study of Intelligence, 2001). Originally classified, the book was declassified in 2009. See cia.gov, FOIA Electronic Reading Room, Vietnam Histories.*

As the Big War Rages, CIA Works at the Insurgency/Hamlet Level

The Tet offensive proved to be an intelligence boon for CIA. The Viet Cong, which had operated underground and in the shadows before the offensive, emerged into the open for the first time to carry out attacks. In doing so, they more clearly revealed numbers, locations, organizational structure, and leadership. As noted above, since the early 1960s, long before the introduction of major US ground forces, the CIA had urged a more intensive effort against the Viet Cong Infrastructure in the South.

One of CIA's chiefs of East Asian operations—and future DCI—William E. Colby was a student of communist guerrilla doctrine, and once noted Mao Zedong's published reference to guerrillas moving among populations like fish in the sea. Colby would assert that a continual US and South Vietnamese effort to remove the guerrilla "fish" from the countryside was a requirement for a stable and secure South Vietnam. Yet CIA lacked the personnel and military support to conduct rural security and pacification efforts on its own. Even after the conclusion of Operation SWITCHBACK in 1963, however, CIA continued working on a much reduced scale with the South Vietnamese to promote development of rural self-defense units, predicated on the idea that arming, organizing, and training the peasantry to act on their own could succeed in wresting control of the countryside from the Viet Cong.

Beginning in April 1964, CIA introduced a scheme that came to be known as the "Oil Spot Approach" to building local security by starting in one small area and working gradually to spread security outward, like a spot

of oil on water. The approach involved creation of small teams deployed throughout the countryside—political action teams, census-grievance teams, and counter-terror teams. The census grievance teams solicited villager concerns about security and the South Vietnamese government while also seeking to identify local Viet Cong cadre. The political action teams then attempted to "rally," or persuade or convert, these local communists to support the South Vietnamese government, or, failing this, refer them to a counter-terror team for apprehension and imprisonment.

CIA and MACV Cooperate in CORDS

This CIA–South Vietnamese initiative remained small until May 1967, when MACV insisted on consolidating all military and civilian pacification efforts into one organization named Civil Operations and Revolutionary Development Support (CORDS). Both CIA and MACV participated in CORDS activities in close cooperation with the government of South Vietnam. MACV for its part created Military Assistance Teams consisting of small groups of US Army soldiers who lived in peasant hamlets, while organizing and training locals to serve in regional and Popular Force militia units to fight communist cells in their local areas, often without the assistance of larger US or South Vietnamese forces. Drawing on the experience of civic action programs undertaken earlier by

Header photo: In 1961, Buon Enao village in Central South Vietnam's Darlac Province was the first village organized for self-defense under the CIDG Program. CIA file photo.

As the Big War Rages, CIA Works at the Insurgency/Hamlet Level

US Marine units in northern South Vietnam, such efforts showed great promise in making a significant difference in the countryside, however slight the Pentagon's support.

CIA veteran Robert Komer directed CORDS from May 1967 until William E. Colby replaced him in 1968. A World War II OSS veteran, Colby joined the CIA in 1950. He served as chief of station in Saigon in 1959 and as chief of the Far Eastern Division starting in 1962. Like McCone and Helms, Colby viewed the bombing of the North and large unit military actions with great skepticism, propounding the theory that eradication of the existing communist parallel government in the South would win over the peasantry and win the war. He believed that allowing any remnants of the enemy to remain active would undermine whatever the US and South Vietnamese governments tried to do.

Under CORDS, CIA concentrated on "winning hearts and minds" through long-overdue land reforms and infrastructure, economic, and agricultural development. It helped direct or redistribute about 2.5 million acres of land from wealthy landowners to the peasants, giving farmers a stake in the future of the nation and a reason to support the South Vietnamese government. CORDS, while working on village defense and civic action programs, also devoted resources to gathering intelligence intended to root out the Viet Cong Infrastructure.

Phoenix

The controversial and largely misunderstood Phoenix Program fell under the broader CORDS umbrella. Although initiated, administered, and ostensibly controlled by the South Vietnamese government, Phoenix received funding and administrative, intelligence, and personnel support from both CIA and MACV. An expansion of the South Vietnamese government's Chieu Hoi or "Open Arms" program created in 1961, Phuong Hoang—or Phoenix—originated in 1967 as a far more intensive and robust anti–Viet Cong initiative with intelligence collection and targeting at its core.

Determining that knowing who was who in the enemy camp comprised a key element of any counterinsurgency program, CIA created the Intelligence Coordination and Exploitation (ICEX) centers at both provincial and district levels—eventually 103 in number. These centers focused on the collection, analysis, and dissemination of intelligence on specific, local members of the Viet Cong, creating individual dossiers on each suspect. There were A, B, C, and D grades of Viet Cong cadre identified through the program as it developed. Those designated as "A's" were the most influential Viet Cong in South Vietnam; the letter "D" categorized the lower-level followers, referred to as "small fry." While the program overwhelmingly collected intelligence and apprehended those in the D categories (small fry being more prevalent), it also recorded successes against top-level members of the Viet Cong Infrastructure.

Dossiers created in the intelligence centers went to the various Phoenix field forces, which included Provincial Reconnaissance Units (PRUs), composed of Navy SEALs, Marines, and Army special operations groups, and CIA-directed and -led Vietnamese, Thai, and Chinese mercenary units, the Vietnamese National Police, and South Vietnamese Army Special Forces. These teams operated in the countryside, patrolling the villages and hamlets, attempting to identify and locate named individuals for apprehension and interrogation at the ICEX centers. The program emphasized the capture—not killing—of suspects, a canard advanced and perpetuated by critics of the war and protesters. Initially, CIA, with Vietnamese assistance, handled interrogations at the ICEX. In 1971, the South Vietnamese government took over all aspects of the program as CIA and US military participation ended. All told, about 600 Americans were directly involved in the interrogation of Viet Cong suspects in the ICEX, including both CIA and US military personnel.

Provincial Reconnaissance Units

The PRUs proved controversial. These special paramilitary units, originally developed in 1964 by the South Vietnamese government and CIA and known initially as the Counter-Terror Teams, eventually numbered some 3,000 members. Critics of US involvement in Vietnam referred to the PRUs as nothing more than targeted assassination teams. Yet PRU actions accounted for only 14 percent of those killed under the Phoenix Program. Indeed, most died in skirmishes and raids involving South Vietnamese soldiers and police and the US military. "A"-level Viet Cong leaders generally

As the Big War Rages, CIA Works at the Insurgency/Hamlet Level

operated with an armed entourage and rarely submitted meekly to arrest or detention when PRUs confronted them. Firefights generally ensued as the result of any encounter, with the inevitable fatalities.

According to CIA figures, Phoenix succeeded in eliminating some 30,000 members of the Viet Cong infrastructure. US Army estimates of VCI losses during this period are even greater. Phoenix and Tet, MACV noted, in conjunction with other rural security and militia programs, eliminated more than 80,000 Viet Cong in South Vietnam. Phoenix activities and pacification programs also succeeded in driving the remnants of the Viet Cong deep underground or into Cambodian or Laotian sanctuaries where their ability to affect events in South Vietnam declined precipitously by the time of the 1972 Easter offensive.

Communist leaders later confirmed the effectiveness of the Phoenix Program and its debilitating effect on the Viet Cong. Communist forces involved in the 1972 Easter offensive and the Final Offensive in 1975 consisted entirely of North Vietnamese regulars operating without Viet Cong assistance, the latter rendered ineffective as a political or military force.

The Hamlet Evaluation System

The Hamlet Evaluation System (HES) adopted by MACV in October 1966 at the suggestion of National Security Advisor Walt Rostow also grew out of CIA's earlier Census Grievance Program. Intended to measure the effect of all US-supported pacification and military activity based on six criteria, it represented an effort to create a national scorecard of progress in winning the war. Following his appointment to CORDS, Colby placed an increased emphasis on the HES to show patterns and trends. The Army did all the legwork. Soldiers went into the hamlets and villages of South Vietnam using a series of surveys and spot checks in an attempt to quantify the progress of rural security and pacification programs in the various locales.

The Army took the surveys as proof of progress. Between 1970 and 1972, they revealed that a good majority of villages in the South finally had come under government control with allegedly 97 percent rated at least "moderately secure," with half rated even higher.

Critics of the system pointed out, however, that hamlet chieftains typically would tell survey teams what they thought the teams wanted to hear, and the moment they had left, the Viet Cong would return and reestablish their control. The overwhelming weight of evidence nonetheless indicates that CIA's efforts did succeed in making the South Vietnamese countryside more secure after 1968.

CIA Technology in the War

CIA-developed technology played an enormous role in intelligence collection and support to the US military effort in Southeast Asia. In 1966, CIA's Technical Services Division (TSD) developed a way to identify individuals who may have recently fired weapons or used explosives. Specialists employed a test for trace contamination that occurs when a person handles a metal object or explosive substance. Placed on the skin or clothing of a Viet Cong suspect, the chemicals would confirm recent firearm use or explosives contact. TSD declassified these "gunshot residue" tests in 1971 and shared the technology with US law enforcement agencies and some foreign intelligence services. TSD developed a wide variety of beacons and sensors to mark bombing targets and landing or exfiltration zones and to detect movement in the jungle or along the Ho Chi Minh Trail. It also designed a variety of tripwire mines, flares, and alarms to assist with perimeter defense.

An aspect of technical support only recently made public was the work of a TSD officer who devised measures that allowed US POWs held in North Vietnam to exchange messages with US military officials in the United States. These communications provided insights into the identities of POWs, conditions within POW camps, and even escape plans.

Between May 1967 and May 1968, the CIA-developed supersonic aircraft, the A-12 Archangel, made appearances over the theater. In its short lifespan, the A-12 provided reconnaissance of North Vietnamese air defenses and troop deployments, until it was replaced by the Air Force variant, the SR-71 Blackbird.

As the Big War Rages, CIA Works at the Insurgency/Hamlet Level

The Approaching End of the War

In the fall of 1972 and early 1973, Henry Kissinger, the advisor to the president for national security affairs (and later secretary of state), was instrumental in secret negotiations ending US involvement in Vietnam, although to critics, the Paris Peace Accords of January 1973 left too many communist troops in the South. Following the agreement, Kissinger and President Nixon promised South Vietnamese President Nguyen Van Thieu that if North Vietnam committed wholesale violations of the settlement, the United States would respond with aerial bombardment and increased aid. However, when Nixon resigned in August 1974 in the wake of the Watergate Affair, the guarantees made to Thieu went with him.

Many in the CIA felt, as did analyst Frank Snepp, that the peace accords created a deliberate "decent interval," a period between US withdrawal in 1973 and an eventual South Vietnamese collapse that would absolve the United States of any direct responsibility for its fall to communism. The debates over whether the decent interval ever existed still rages among historians today, in spite of decades of denials from policymakers serving at the time.

Studies Selections:

Elkes, Martin C. "The LAMS Story." *Studies in Intelligence* 19, no. 2 (1975): 29–34. Originally SECRET—Released in part.

Finlayson, Andrew R. "The Tay Ninh Provincial Reconnaissance Unit and Its Role in the Phoenix Program, 1969–70." *Studies in Intelligence* 51, no. 2 (2007): 59–69. Originally UNCLASSIFIED.

Leidesdorf, Titus. "The Vietnamese as Operational Target." *Studies in Intelligence* 12, no. 4 (1968): 57–71. Originally SECRET—Released in full.

Linder, James C. "The Fall of Lima Site 85." *Studies in Intelligence* 38, no. 4 (1994): 43–52. Originally UNCLASSIFIED. Reprinted with updating editor's note and new afterword in *Studies in Intelligence* 59, no. 1 (March 2015).

Mark, David. "The Mayaguez Rescue Operation Revisited." *Studies in Intelligence* 23, no. 2 (1979): 29–32. Originally SECRET//NOFORN—Released in full.

Maximov, William J. and Edward Scrutchings. "The Metal Traces Test." *Studies in Intelligence* 11, no. 4 (1967): 37–44. Originally CONFIDENTIAL//NOFORN—Released in full.

Peterson, Gordon I. and David C. Taylor. "A Shield and Sword: Intelligence Support to Communications with US POWs in Vietnam," *Studies in Intelligence* 60, no. 1 (2016): 1–16. Originally UNCLASSIFIED.

Pribbenow, Merle L. "The Man in the Snow White Cell." *Studies in Intelligence* 48, no. 1 (2004): 59–69. Originally UNCLASSIFIED.

Mrs. and Ambassador Ellsworth Bunker in 1967 deplaning from an Air America aircraft to visit the US mission in Vung Tau in the southern portion of South Vietnam. CIA file photo.

Helio-Courier on the ground in Laos. The aircraft was better suited to mountain flying than helicopters, but it was demanding to fly. CIA file photo.

MPG 58625AI 3-68

From Thomas L Ahern, Jr., Undercover Armies: CIA and Surrogate Warfare in Laos *(Center for the Studiy of Intelligence, 2006). Originally classified, the book was declassified in large part and released in 2009. See cia.gov Freedom of Information Act Reading Room.*

Meanwhile, CIA in Laos, 1954-74

Throughout the Vietnam War, CIA played a major role in a related conflict in Laos. The US can date its initial involvement in Laos to mid-1954, but its large-scale covert action effort began in 1960. The effort primarily involved support to the Laotian government and the organization of paramilitary units among the Hmong hill peoples. The Hmong were rural slash-and-burn subsistence farmers who had supported the French throughout the colonial period. They had fought the Japanese during World War II, and they despised the Viet Minh after the war.

CIA support to Laos began with financial aid given between 1954 and 1959 to a rightwing general named Phoumi Nousavan, who took control of the government after the 1954 Geneva Conference granted independence to Laos (and divided Vietnam). Nevertheless, by 1960, opposition to Nousavan had grown. Souvanna Phouma, a neutralist, and Souphanouvong, a communist, combined their forces against Nousavan.

President Dwight D. Eisenhower said, "We cannot let Laos fall to the communists even if we have to fight." But Nousavan remained too weak and unpopular to save. Although 5,000 US troops were in nearby Thailand in 1960, President John F. Kennedy chose a diplomatic solution rather than risk a military conflict in Laos.

In May 1961, during a conference in Geneva, US Ambassador W. Averill Harriman arranged an agreement creating a neutral Laos, with Souvanna Phouma at the head of a coalition government that included Souphaouvong and the communist Pathet Lao. The agreement also called for the removal of all foreign forces

from Laos, reflecting President Kennedy's view that Laos was remote and not vital to US interests.

Language of the agreement also called for the removal of North Vietnamese forces, which were then moving personnel and supplies down the Ho Chi Minh Trail into South Vietnam. Although the United States withdrew its military forces from Laos, establishing a demilitarized zone, the North Vietnamese did not because Laos remained vital as an infiltration route into South Vietnam.

The Objective: Interdiction Along the Ho Chi Minh Trail

Eventually, US leaders began to see that the interdiction of communist men and supplies on this route was essential to a growing effort to stabilize South Vietnam. Therefore, CIA began a covert effort to harass the North Vietnamese with the assistance of the Hmong and Laotians. They replaced the overt presence of US Special Forces who had previously performed the same mission and added interdiction and intelligence collection to harassment operations.

CIA also recognized early that while it could cause problems for the North Vietnamese on the Ho Chi Minh Trail in Laos, it could not eradicate the communist influence in the country. At the same time, the North Vietnamese goal was limited to keeping the Ho Chi Minh Trail open. As a result of this curious confluence of

Header photo: Hmong paramilitary operations in Laos were led and supplied from Long Tieng, which grew during the conflict from a barely inhabited village in 1961 to a population center of nearly 30,000 people. CIA file photo.

Meanwhile, CIA in Laos, 1954–74

interests, CIA paramilitary officers would wage a classic low-intensity conflict aimed at the North Vietnamese that neither side wanted to escalate.

Eventually, CIA led an army of about 40,000 Hmong fighters under General Vang Pao. This low-level war succeeded in harassing the North Vietnamese on the Ho Chi Minh Trail, but declining morale among the Hmong coincided with increased communist activities in Laos after 1968, when North Vietnamese Army forces took on a more direct military role in South Vietnam after the Tet offensive.

Air America's Role

CIA also focused on supplying the Hmong and other anti-communist forces with food, medicine, and military aid delivered by the proprietary airline Air America. Founded in 1958, Air America eventually consisted of a fleet of 30 helicopters, 24 twin-engine transports, and two dozen short-takeoff-and-landing aircraft. The aircraft operated from sites in the interior of Laos and in northern Thailand. Air America inserted and extracted road watch teams and flew night airdrop missions of personnel, supplies, and sensors over the Ho Chi Minh Trail. It also performed search-and-rescue missions to retrieve downed US fliers. Additionally, Air America pilots conducted some highly successful photoreconnaissance missions over North Vietnam and Laos. During this period, Air America made possible numerous clandestine missions conducted by US Special Forces.

The Beginning of the End

A February 1974 cease-fire agreement led to the formation of a new coalition government in Laos that involved both the US-backed royalist government and the North Vietnamese–backed Pathet Lao. It proved to be a short-lived peace. In 1975 after the fall of South Vietnam and Cambodia, the Laotian communists pushed the Royalists out of power and seized the government. The Hmong continued fighting well into 1975, but they did so without the support of the United States, which had ended its commitment to Southeast Asia. During the Laotian war, about 17,000 tribesmen died. Ninety-seven Air America pilots and crewmembers also lost their lives. The last Air America aircraft and the last CIA officers left Laos in June 1974.

Studies Selections:

Absher, Kenneth Michael. "John Kearns and the Cold War in Laos." *Studies in Intelligence* 46, no. 4 (2002): 45–54. Originally SECRET//NOFORN—Released in part.

Castle, Timothy. "From the Bay of Pigs to Laos— Operation MILLPOND: The Beginning of a Distant Covert War." *Studies in Intelligence* 59, no. 2 (2015): 1–16. Originally UNCLASSIFIED.

Holm, Richard L. "Recollections of a Case Officer in Laos, 1962–1964." *Studies in Intelligence* 47, no. 1 (2003): 1–17. Originally UNCLASSIFIED.

Leary, William M. "CIA Air Operations in Laos, 1955– 1974." *Studies in Intelligence* 42, no. 2 (1998): 71–86. Originally UNCLASSIFIED.

McCann, Frederic. "Gathering Intelligence in Laos in 1968." *Studies in Intelligence* 49, no. 1 (2005): 27–31. Originally UNCLASSIFIED.

Petchell, Robert A. "Cash on Delivery." *Studies in Intelligence* 17, no. 3 (1973): 1–7. Originally SECRET— Released in part.

Stockinger, Edwin K. "Five Weeks at Phalane." *Studies in Intelligence* 17, no. 1 (1973): 11–19. Originally SECRET// NOFORN—Released in part.

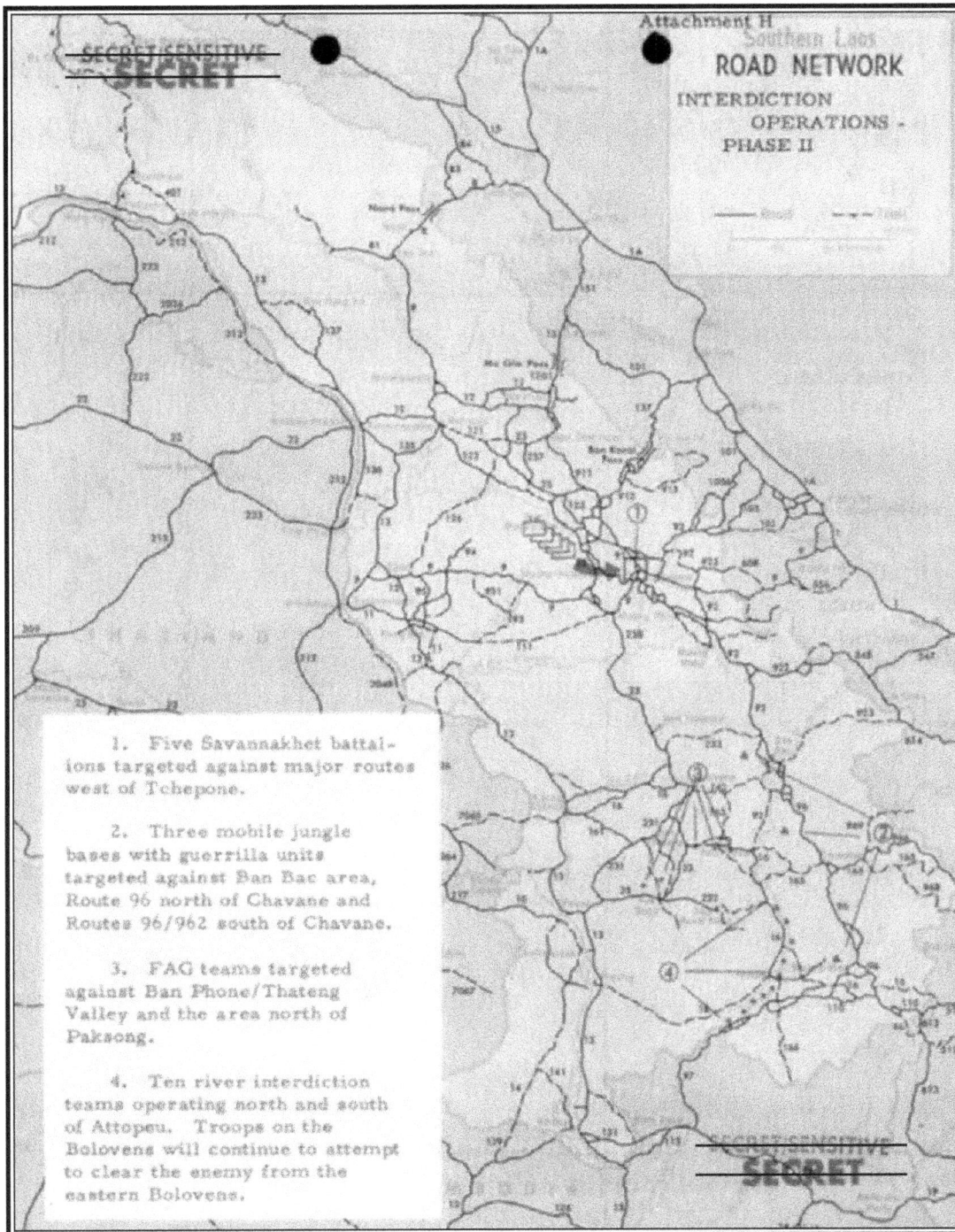

Map showing locations of planned interdiction efforts along the Ho Chi Minh Trail in 1970. Map from Thomas L. Ahern, Jr., Undercover Armies: CIA and Surrogate Warfare in Laos.

Above photo: A Hmong village ca. 1964. CIA officers leading the Hmong army saw helping their people preserve their ways of life as part of the covert project. CIA file photo.

Left photo: A Hmong soldier in an undated CIA photo heads home, chicken in hand. The evacuation from Laos of Hmong fighters after 1975 posed serious challenges for CIA and other US government agencies. CIA file photo.

Postwar Reflections

The Southeast Asian conflict gave birth to an enormous literature reflecting on the conflict's aim and purposes and detailing through memoir and historical research the military and diplomatic actions of all sides. Inevitably, discussion of lessons of the era would find their way into the pages of *Studies*. A few, the earliest or those written by important players of the period, reflecting mainly on leadership and overall Intelligence Community analysis, are included in this collection.

Studies Selections:

Allen, George W. "Intelligence in Small Wars." *Studies in Intelligence* 35, no. 4 (1991): 19–27. Originally UNCLASSIFIED.

Bunker, Ellsworth. "Vietnam in Retrospect." *Studies in Intelligence* 18, no. 1 (1974): 41–47. Originally CONFIDENTIAL—Released in full.

Ford, Harold P. "Thoughts Engendered by Robert McNamara's 'In Retrospect.'" *Studies in Intelligence* 39, no. 1 (1995): 95–109. Originally UNCLASSIFIED.

———, "Why CIA Analysts Were So Doubtful About Vietnam." *Studies in Intelligence* 40, no. 2 (1996): 43–53. Originally UNCLASSIFIED.

———, "William Colby: Retrospect." *Studies in Intelligence* 40, no. 1 (1996): 1–5. Originally UNCLASSIFIED.

Hathaway, Robert M. "Richard Helms as DCI." *Studies in Intelligence* 37, no. 4 (1993): 33–40. Originally SECRET—Released in full.

Laurie, Clayton. "Intelligence in Public Literature, Takes on Intelligence and the Vietnam War," *Studies in Intelligence* 55, no. 2 (2011): 73–77. Originally UNCLASSIFIED.

Lewis, Anthony Marc. "Re-examining Our Perceptions on Vietnam." *Studies in Intelligence* 17, no. 4 (1973): 1–62. Original SECRET—Released in full.

Header photo: US civilians being evacuated from Saigon in April 1975. DOD photo.

Annotated Selections

The annotations to articles below are arranged according to the sections of the historical overview in which the articles were initially cited. While the articles cited in Part I are shown within each section in formal bibliographic style (by author name), those annotated below were curated to track roughly chronologically with historical events as they unfolded (rather than by author name or publication date). Each article is hyperlinked to a PDF in the web. The PDFs are located in the public website of CIA's Center for the Study of Intelligence.

Indochina–In Support of a Colonial Power, 1945–54

Swift, Carleton A., Richard D. Kovar, and Russell J. Bowen. **"Intelligence in Recent Public Literature: *Why Vietnam? Prelude to America's Albatross*."** *Studies in Intelligence* 25, no. 2 (1981): 99–116. Originally UNCLASSIFIED.

While President Harry Truman may very well have shared many of President Franklin Roosevelt's perceptions and beliefs, the need to include France as a member of NATO and the Cold War alliance against the Soviet Union muted any qualms he or American critics may have had about supporting a French return to their former colony after it was liberated from the Japanese. With the outbreak of the first Indochina War in 1946—and through the French defeat and withdrawal in 1954—few questioned the need for ever increasing amounts of economic, military, diplomatic, and intelligence aid to the French in Indochina. One who did so, though belatedly in public, was the OSS officer who first met Ho Chi Minh, Archimedes Patti. The title of his memoir of OSS service in Indochina at the end of WWII and in months after spoke loudly to that doubt. This collection of reviews published in Studies *in 1981 includes the work of two reviewers who were participants in the evolution of CIA involvement in Southeast Asia. One, Carleton Swift, replaced Patti as chief of Hanoi Station. Both bring in personal experience and perspective.*

LePage, Jean-Marc and Elie Tenenbaum. **"French and American Intelligence Relations During the First Indochina War, 1950–1954."** *Studies in Intelligence* 55, no. 3 (2011): 19–27. Originally UNCLASSIFIED.

As French scholars Jean-Marc LePage and Elie Tenenbaum recount, relationships between French intelligence and security organizations operating in Indochina with the CIA mirrored patterns and behaviors seen elsewhere from the top policy levels in the French, Vietnamese, and US capitals to the Southeast Asian battlefields. Periods of intelligence cooperation and sharing alternated with times of estrangement, exclusion, and secrecy on both sides.

The Republic of Vietnam, Insurgency and Nation-Building, 1954–65

Palmer, Gen. Bruce. **"US Intelligence and Vietnam."** *Studies in Intelligence* 28, no. 5 (Special Issue, 1984). Originally SECRET//NOFORN—Released in part.

West Point graduate, career US Army officer, with distinguished service during World War II, in Korea and in the Dominican Republic, Gen. Bruce Palmer, Jr., commanded II Field Force in Vietnam, beginning in 1966. He served from May 1967 to August 1968 as the deputy commanding general of the US Army–Vietnam. Several years after Palmer's military retirement in August 1974, DCI Stansfield Turner appointed Palmer to a position on the Central Intelligence Agency Senior Review Panel, on which the general served for five years. Possessing in-depth knowledge of military and intelligence affairs, Palmer was asked in 1982 by CSI and by the Directorate of Intelligence to study CIA intelligence products relating to the Vietnam conflict. Palmer's originally classified study appeared in 1984 and remains one of the best and most comprehensive works on the Agency's intelligence collection and analytical roles in Vietnam. Intended as an in-house teaching tool for training future intelligence analysts, Palmer's study neither glorifies CIA successes nor covers up its failures.

Ahern, Thomas L. Jr. **"The CIA and the Government of Ngo Dinh Diem."** *Studies in Intelligence* 37, no. 4 (1993): 41–51. Originally SECRET—Released in part.

A noncommunist alternative to Ho Chi Minh did exist in Ngo Dinh Diem, a nationalist, Western-educated Catholic previously designated by the French as the prime minister of Vietnam under Emperor Bao Dai. Diem, however, did not possess Ho's charisma or popularity, and in 1954, Diem did not effectively control even southern Vietnam, let alone any territory or significant population north of the 17th Parallel. In order to stabilize Diem's fledgling government—a government that faced myriad rivals and contenders from French-backed generals, religious sects, and local warlords—the Eisenhower administration called on the CIA. As CIA Historian Thomas Ahern notes, "The same combination of goal-oriented action and intellectual objectivity that CIA officers brought to bear" in this case, "also produced pioneering work on the operational concepts and techniques of interagency coordination that later defined the American counterinsurgency effort in Vietnam." Ahern would build on this early work to publish within CIA four book-length histories of US engagement in Southeast Asia. These and two other monographs were redacted and released in 2009. They are available in the Freedom of Information Act Electronic Reading Room of www.cia.gov under the headings Historical Collections/Vietnam Histories. Future mentions of this work will simply refer to "Ahern Vietnam Histories."

Allen, George W. **"Covering Coups in Saigon."** *Studies in Intelligence* 33, no. 4 (1989): 57–61. Originally SECRET—Released in part.

Despite US efforts at nation-building and political stabilization, embattled and deteriorating South Vietnamese regimes experienced more than a dozen coups, leadership reshuffles, and other crises in just over a five-year period beginning in late 1960. The coup that toppled Ngo Dinh Diem in November 1963 and led to his death and that of his brother, Ngo Dinh Nhu, began a series of revolving-door governments

The Republic of Vietnam, Insurgency and Nation-Building, 1954–65

composed of military strongmen and weak civilian politicians during the next four years, just as CIA analysts and DCI John McCone had predicted. Through it all, the CIA's Saigon Station, staffed with analysts and operations officers, kept policymakers in Washington, DC, and in the US Country Team at the Saigon embassy abreast of political and military developments as they occurred, providing a continuous, accurate, and comprehensive picture of events on the ground.

Hartness, William M. **"Aspects of Counterinsurgency Intelligence."** *Studies in Intelligence* 7, no. 4 (1963): 71–83. Originally CONFIDENTIAL—Released in full and reprinted in *Studies in Intelligence* 58, no. 4 (2015).

In a US military establishment just beginning to recognize the requirements for fighting low-intensity conflicts, US Army Lt. Col. William M. Hartness identified in this 1963 article the importance of intelligence, especially before the advent of any conflict or operation. He encouraged Area Studies, or basic surveys of the operational areas—geography, sociocultural, political, economic, and military—long before intervention. Once aware of the environment, this assessment would serve as the basis for counterinsurgency operational planning to include preventive, reactive, aggressive, and remedial measures. While sound in concept, there is little evidence indicating that MACV acted upon these suggestions at the time or after the commitment of US ground forces to Vietnam in March 1965.

Matthias, Willard C. **"How Three Estimates Went Wrong."** *Studies in Intelligence* 12, no. 1 (1968): 27–38. Originally SECRET//NOFORN—Released in part.

Collecting and analyzing intelligence to provide the most accurate independent assessments of the world situation in the form of National Intelligence Estimates (NIEs) to the president and policymaker is a primary CIA mission. The CIA's Board of National Estimates, created in 1950, held responsibility for this important function during the Vietnam War era and worked with more than 11 other Defense and Intelligence Community members of the United States Intelligence Board (USIB) to produce coordinated findings. As a CIA board member, Willard C. Matthias explains that this process could often produce significant changes in the substance, tone, and conclusions of any given initial estimate, resulting in the delivery of an intelligence viewpoint contrary to the reality on the ground or what the CIA Estimates Staff and Board may have originally intended. Only one of the three estimates addressed in this article dealt with Vietnam—Prospects in South Vietnam, NIE 53-63, 17 April 1963. This estimate and a multitude of others are reproduced in Estimative Products on Vietnam, 1948–1975. The collection was produced by the National Intelligence Council in April 2005. Like the Ahern Vietnam Histories, it is available in the CIA's public, Freedom of Information Act Electronic Reading Room under the headings Historical Collections/NIC Vietnam Collection.

Schiattareggia, M. H. **"Counterintelligence in Counter-Guerrilla Operations."** *Studies in Intelligence* 6, no. 3 (1962): 1–24. Originally SECRET—Released in full and reprinted in *Studies in Intelligence* 57, No. 2 (June 2013): 39–63.

The Republic of Vietnam, Insurgency and Nation-Building, 1954–65

By the end of 1962, the Kennedy administration had committed more than 11,000 military advisers to training and assisting the military and police forces of the Republic of South Vietnam. The CIA had also committed several score officers to raising, training, and directing rural militia units in antiguerrilla warfare, most successfully in Vietnam's central highlands. US forces would find a different type of conflict than anything they had seen before. To US military leaders, accustomed to large-scale conventional conflicts, counterguerrilla warfare, low intensity conflict, and counterinsurgency as it developed in Southeast Asia was relatively new. Schiattareggia surveys the classics of guerrilla warfare literature produced by its most famous theorists to that time, those who would become household names to Americans during the war. Knowing how one's adversaries think and operate, the author maintains, is the first step toward defeating them.

Schwarzchild, Edward T. **"The Assessment of Insurgency."** *Studies in Intelligence* 7, no. 4 (1963): 85–89. Originally SECRET—Released in full.

Making sense of the overwhelming amount of raw data collected on any given issue and then determining what is most useful to the commander or policymaker is one of the intelligence analysts' most central and daunting tasks. Edward T. Schwarzchild, writing in the fall of 1963, describes the difficulties of those collecting increasing amounts of information about the growing insurgency in South Vietnam. Schwarzchild stressed, "Counterinsurgency is extraordinary, posing intelligence problems too large, too complicated, too detailed, and too fast-moving to be handled by procedures designed for other times and other information."

Smith, Russell Jack. **"Intelligence Production During the Helms Regime."** *Studies in Intelligence* 39, no. 4 (1995): 93–102. Originally SECRET—Released in part.

During Richard Helms's tenure as DCI, analytical reporting to the president had matured and regularized, reaching the White House in the form of National Intelligence Estimates and in the various publications of the Directorate of Intelligence, including memoranda and the President's Daily Brief. The NIEs had become a routine series, broad in scope, although they could deal with short-term or contingency matters. DI memoranda tended to deal with analysis of long-range trends. As Russell Jack Smith, the deputy director of intelligence during this time wrote, Helms took an active interest in the quality and timeliness of NIEs and other reporting that appeared at the White House, at NSC meetings, and on the desk of Secretary of Defense Robert S. McNamara and others at the Pentagon.

Steinmeyer, Walter. **"The Intelligence Role in Counterinsurgency."** *Studies in Intelligence* 9, no. 4 (1965): 57–63. Originally SECRET—Released in full and reprinted in *Studies in Intelligence* 59, no. 4 (December 2015).

In January 1961, Soviet Communist Party General Secretary Nikita Khrushchev promised the full cooperation and support of the communist USSR to worldwide "wars of national liberation," defined as "struggles by all colonies and dependent countries against international imperialism" and as "uprisings against rotten reactionary regimes." In practice, however, as Walter Steinmeyer—the penname of

The Republic of Vietnam, Insurgency and Nation-Building, 1954–65

senior Directorate of Operations officer Theodore Shackley—wrote, the Soviets and their communist Chinese and Cuban allies sought to "exploit for their own purposes dissension, turmoil, and impatience for reform in Latin America, Africa, the Near East, and Southeast Asia," through aggression against fledgling or weak democracies, recently independent former colonies, or economically depressed areas aligned with the United States. The greatest national security challenge facing the United States in this era of nuclear stalemate, Steinmeyer thus asserted, was of confronting communist subversion and totalitarianism hiding behind the guise of benevolent "national liberation" movements.

The War "Goes Big," 1965–75

Ford, Harold P. **"The US Decision to Go Big in Vietnam."** *Studies in Intelligence* 29, no. 1 (1985): 1–15. Originally SECRET//NOFORN—Released in full.

In the crucial years of 1962 to 1965, CIA's Harold Ford, who served as chief of the Far East Staff, and then as the chief, Estimates Staff, Office of National Estimates, held a direct advisory role in relation to US policymakers grappling with the growing communist insurgency in South Vietnam. In the aftermath of the coup against Ngo Dinh Diem in November 1963, the situation in South Vietnam grew ever more precarious, prompting those within the Johnson administration to consider a larger military commitment and expansion of the war to North Vietnam, then seen as the source of the conflict. In this article, Ford describes CIA involvement with policymakers debating whether to "go big" in Vietnam in 1964 and 1965 by bombing North Vietnam and dispatching sizable ground forces and what impact intelligence assessments did, or did not have, on those decisions. Ford explored these themes in greater detail in CIA and the Vietnam Policymakers: Three Episodes, 1962–1968, *which was published by CSI in 1998. The complete work is available on CSI's page in www.cia.gov.*

Atkins, Merle, Kenneth C. Fuller, and Bruce Smith. **"'Rolling Thunder' and Bomb Damage to Bridges."** *Studies in Intelligence* 13, no. 4 (1969): 1–9. Originally SECRET//NOFORN—Released in full.

Once the Johnson administration made the decision to "go big" in Vietnam, the Rolling Thunder bombing campaign of North Vietnam proved a major component of the new effort. Based on the erroneous policy assessment that military pressure on North Vietnam in the form of a gradually escalating, yet restrained, air campaign would convince communist leaders to end assistance to the insurgency in the South and negotiate a settlement, the air war began on 2 March 1965. During the next three years in an on-again, off-again fashion, air units from three services pounded portions of North Vietnam's scant transportation and industrial infrastructure. As Atkins, Fuller, and Smith recount, "As the days of the air campaign over North Vietnam stretched into months, the requirement developed in Washington and particularly the White House for independent assessments of the results." CIA analysts teamed up with analysts from the three-year-old Defense Intelligence Agency to produce coordinated assessments.

The War "Goes Big," 1965–75

Hall, Arthur B. **"Landscape Analysis."** *Studies in Intelligence* 11, no. 3 (1967): 65–75. Originally SECRET//NOFORN—Released in full.

Intelligence comes in many shapes and forms. During the Vietnam era, CIA collected geographic intelligence, not as an exercise to create cartographic products, although the Agency did have such a branch, but to "analyze the distribution of things on the earth's surface as they relate to the formulation and execution of US policy." As Arthur Hall relates, initially the geographic intelligence or landscape analysis developed within CIA made major contributions to bombing and interdiction campaigns along the Ho Chi Minh Trail in Laos and Cambodia. In this context, he noted, the geographic analyst could determine vulnerable points in the transportation network and the most effective bombing points.

Puchalla, Edward F. **"Communist Defense Against Aerial Surveillance in Southeast Asia."** *Studies in Intelligence* 14, no. 2 (1970): 31–78. Originally SECRET//NOFORN—Released in full.

Most every intelligence or military innovation developed in wartime will typically provide only temporary advantage as adversaries devise countermeasures, if not leap ahead with innovations of their own. Edward F. Puchalla wrote of this concept in the context of the Rolling Thunder and air interdiction campaigns conducted by the United States in North and South Vietnam, Cambodia, and Laos between 1964 and 1968. The communists, especially in North Vietnam, sought to lessen the impact of the bombing through ever more sophisticated and clever concealments, decoys, dispersions, and deceptions.

Sinclair, Robert, **"One Intelligence Analyst Remembers Another: A Review of *Who the Hell Are We Fighting? The Story of Sam Adams and the Vietnam Intelligence Wars*."** *Studies in Intelligence* 50, No. 4 (2006): 1–9. Originally UNCLASSIFIED.

Robert Sinclair, himself a CIA analyst with Sam Adams during the Vietnam War, used his review of Michael Hiam's 2006 biography of Adams to detail the challenges of presenting and defending CIA's unpopular estimates of North Vietnamese and Viet Cong strengths in the face of the countervailing views of the Department of Defense and the US military hierarchy. A good many analysts in CIA and the military agreed that official military estimates were too low, but only Sam Adams kept fighting after 1967, when the issue was defined away in the key National Intelligence Estimate discussed above. In the review, Sinclair goes on to reflect on the lessons for analysts in the pressurized environment of the time.

Kitchens, Allen H. **"Crisis and Intelligence: Two Case Studies [Tet and Iran]."** *Studies in Intelligence* 28, No. 3 (1984): 71–78. Originally UNCLASSIFIED.

The communist Tet offensive in January 1968 proved a turning point in the Vietnam War. Although a stunning military defeat for North Vietnam and their southern Viet Cong allies, it proved a psychological victory because of the very recent optimistic public predictions of an impending US victory that had been made by the Johnson administration. In the immediate aftermath of the offensive, military leaders in South Vietnam and policymakers in Washington drew the ire of antiwar critics. In turn, the

The War "Goes Big," 1965–75

CIA drew criticism for an alleged intelligence failure, neglecting to provide timely and actionable indications and warning. In the case of Tet, the intelligence remained fragmentary, policymakers and commanders "had been lulled into a false sense of security," and most anticipated that any offensive would "follow traditional lines."

Tidwell, William A. **"A New Kind of Air Targeting."** *Studies in Intelligence* 11, no. 1 (1967): 55–60. Originally CONFIDENTIAL//NOFORN—Released in full.

Since its founding, the primary mission of the Central Intelligence Agency has been collecting information on real and potential adversaries' motivations, plans, and intentions and then producing analyzed, actionable intelligence for the policymaker and warfighter. Although providing intelligence in support of the military did not figure prominently in the CIA's chartering documents, the CIA did come to provide increased assistance in theory and in fact during the wars in Southeast Asia. In this article, William Tidwell describes how intelligence can prove invaluable in targeting and destroying an insurgency in its early stages.

As the Big War Rages, CIA Works at the Insurgency/Hamlet Level

Finlayson, Andrew R. **"The Tay Ninh Provincial Reconnaissance Unit and Its Role in the Phoenix Program, 1969–70."** *Studies in Intelligence* 51, no. 2 (2007): 59–69. Originally UNCLASSIFIED.

As retired US Marine Col. Andrew Finlayson writes, "The Phoenix Program is arguably the most misunderstood and controversial program undertaken by the governments of the United States and South Vietnam during the Vietnam War." Antiwar critics at the time, and numbers of historians since, portray the program that aimed to eradicate the communist parallel government in South Vietnam, known as the Viet Cong Infrastructure, as an "unlawful and immoral assassination program targeting civilians." As the author describes, however, the Phoenix Program was an intelligence collection program, one that CIA had worked to develop and implement for many years in cooperation with the South Vietnamese government that sought to identify Viet Cong cadre and rank-and-file fighters with the goal of removing them from the fight through persuasion or capture.

Elkes, Martin C. **"The LAMS Story."** *Studies in Intelligence* 19, no. 2 (1975): 29–34. Originally SECRET—Released in part.

Intelligence officers often require specialized equipment that must be purpose-built. In other cases, however, existing technology can be adapted for intelligence use. During the wars in Southeast Asia, CIA officers needed low-cost and accurate position locating, communications, and navigation gear capable of working at multiple altitudes on land and at sea in varying terrain, climate, and weather conditions. In 1967, representatives from several CIA offices, including the Office of the Special Assistant for Vietnamese Affairs (SAVA), the Special Operations Division (SOD), the Technical Services Division (TSD), and the Office of Research and Development (ORD), developed requirements for a device meeting Agency needs. Based on the US Air

As the Big War Rages, CIA Works at the Insurgency/Hamlet Level

Force Long Range Navigation, or LORAN, the system adapted for use became known as the LAMS, or LORAN Airborne Modular System.

Leidesdorf, Titus. **"The Vietnamese as Operational Target."** *Studies in Intelligence* 12, no. 4 (1968): 57–71. Originally SECRET—Released in full.

From statesmen, to soldiers, to intelligence officers, Americans often displayed, and often noted, their lack of in-depth knowledge of Vietnam, its culture and history, and especially understanding of its people—peasants or elites, military or political leaders, in either the North or the South. Psychologist Titus Leidesdorf rejected this idea of the inscrutable Vietnamese, who "project the image of a homogenous people, proud of their heritage and their ethnic superiority and . . . sense of unbroachable [sic] unity." He noted they were actually quite the opposite and as a people they were extraordinarily diverse and could be classified into a variety of regional, social, political, class and ideological groupings, adhering to various organizational and ideological behaviors, all discernable and ultimately exploitable.

Linder, James C. **"The Fall of Lima Site 85."** *Studies in Intelligence* 38, no. 4 (1994): 43–52. Originally UNCLASSIFIED. Reprinted with updating editor's note and new afterword in *Studies in Intelligence* 59, no. 1 (March 2015).

James C. Linder provides one of the earliest public accounts given of the successful North Vietnamese attack in early 1968 on Lima Site 85, a remote mountaintop US installation near the Laotian–North Vietnamese border. By 1965, US policy in Laos had evolved into a covert war waged by CIA against the communist Pathet Lao and their North Vietnamese allies, who used the nearby Ho Chi Minh Trail to transport men and supplies to the war in South Vietnam. Lima Site 85 was built in August 1966 on a 5,600-foot-tall mountain named Phou Phathi, 100 miles south of Dien Bien Phu. It served as a Tactical Air Navigation (TACAN) station to support the growing air interdiction campaign in Laos and the bombing campaign in North Vietnam. The site was operated by US Air Force and Lockheed Corporation technicians and supplied by frequent Air America flights from Udorn, Thailand. Lima 85 had also served as a CIA paramilitary base for Hmong fighters operating in the region. The site served vital tactical and strategic functions in US air operations against North Vietnamese targets, itself becoming a target for urgent North Vietnamese action.

Maximov, William J. and Edward Scrutchings. **"The Metal Traces Test."** *Studies in Intelligence* 11, no. 4 (1967): 37–44. Originally CONFIDENTIAL//NOFORN–Released in full.

DS&T chemists, scientists, technicians, engineers, and craftsmen worked in close cooperation with the Technical Services Division (TSD) of CIA's operations directorate to develop all manner of paraphernalia for use by those dealing in espionage or paramilitary activities, much as their predecessors had done in the World War II Office of Strategic Services. By the mid-1960s, the DS&T not only created purpose-built specialized equipment, but also designed, built, and deployed a growing array of ground, aerial, and space-based technical collection systems. While many S&T products and inventions had possible military uses, it was not until the Vietnam

As the Big War Rages, CIA Works at the Insurgency/Hamlet Level

War that the CIA began to provide specialized technology to the military. One such example, the trace metal detection test, and its later iteration detecting explosives use or "gunshot residue," are readily recognizable by any American who has ever watched a crime drama or police show on television.

Peterson, Gordon I. and David C. Taylor. **"A Shield and Sword: Intelligence Support to Communications with US POWs in Vietnam."** *Studies in Intelligence* 60, no. 1 (2016): 1–16. Originally UNCLASSIFIED.

Another example of CIA technical support to the military was institution of a program of secret communications between Washington and US prisoners of war held in North Vietnam. Composed of secret writing techniques developed years before, the system was devised and carried out at the request of the US military by a single CIA officer, who often worked after normal working hours to perfect secret messages for delivery to prisoners with mail privileges. The system gave Washington information about POW identities, prison conditions, and even escape plans.

Pribbenow, Merle L. **"The Man in the Snow White Cell."** *Studies in Intelligence* 48, no. 1 (2004): 59–69. Originally UNCLASSIFIED.

Retired CIA officer Merle Pribbenow supervised Vietnamese language translation services at Saigon Station during the later years of the Vietnam War. Decades later, during the early post-9/11 years when CIA officers first began to interrogate recalcitrant al-Qa'ida members, he recalled similar difficulties when trying to obtain information from communist adversaries. Pribbenow cites the case of Nguyen Tai, "who turned out to be the most senior North Vietnamese officer ever captured during the Vietnam War," who "resisted years of unrelenting interrogation by some of the CIA's most skilled, and South Vietnam's most brutal, interrogators."

Mark, David. **"The Mayaguez Rescue Operation Revisited."** *Studies in Intelligence* 23, no. 2 (1979): 29–32. Originally SECRET//NOFORN—Released in full.

On 12 May 1975, members of the communist Khmer Rouge seized the US merchant ship Mayaguez in the Gulf of Siam off Cambodia, taking the 39 crewmembers to the small Koh Tang Island, 34 miles south of Kompong Som. When efforts to negotiate the release of the crew failed, President Gerald R. Ford determined that a rescue attempt by US Marines stationed in the Pacific was the only option to prevent movement of the hostages to the mainland and an uncertain fate. When military planners approached the CIA's National Photographic Interpretation Center (NPIC) for information to assist the rescuers, NPIC turned to another small CIA office, the Domestic Collection Division (DCD). DCD maintained "extensive contacts with US oil companies" that possessed the most up-to-date charts, maps, and photographs obtained from petroleum exploration activities, as well as field representatives and engineers. As Mark notes, "a major part of the basic intelligence on which the action rested was provided" by this small office.

Meanwhile, CIA in Laos, 1954–74

Leary, William M. **"CIA Air Operations in Laos, 1955–1974."** *Studies in Intelligence* 42, no. 2 (1998): 71–86. Originally UNCLASSIFIED.

CIA operations in Laos between 1955 and 1974 represented CIA's largest paramilitary operation during the Vietnam War era. The United States first began economic and military aid to the Royal Lao Government in Vientiane in 1950 and then established the United States Operations Mission (USOM) five years later, after the Geneva Conference of 1954 neutralized Laos upon the withdrawal of the French from Indochina. CIA officers belonged to USOM, which, in turn, drew support throughout Laos after 1957 by the CIA's proprietary airline, Civil Air Transport, acquired in 1950. CAT supported covert operations throughout Asia, while ostensibly operating as a typical East Asian commercial airline providing regularly scheduled passenger and freight services. It was renamed Air America in March 1959. Historian William Leary recounts the origins and evolution of the airline in Laos. In the process, he provides an excellent, detailed account of the evolution of CIA's secret war against North Vietnam and the indigenous communist Pathet Lao along the Ho Chi Minh Trail in the eastern portion of the country.

Castle, Timothy. **"From the Bay of Pigs to Laos—Operation MILLPOND: The Beginning of a Distant Covert War."** *Studies in Intelligence* 59, no. 2 (2015): 1–16. Originally UNCLASSIFIED.

In this essay, Timothy N. Castle, an Air Force combat veteran of the Vietnam War turned historian of the wars in Southeast Asia, reflects on the international activism of the John F. Kennedy administration, which simultaneously took on covert military interventions in Cuba and Laos only months after Kennedy was inaugurated in 1961. As the well-known Bay of Pigs operation was under way in April 1961, so too was a joint CIA-Pentagon plan to bomb a communist supply station in Laos. As the assault on Cuba faltered, the Laos airstrikes were canceled just four hours before they were to be launched. Nonetheless, and perhaps unintentionally, the presidentially authorized preparations for Operation MILLPOND became the taproot for what eventually emerged, in one veteran's words, as the "largest, most innovative program of irregular warfare ever conducted by CIA."

Holm, Richard L. **"Recollections of a Case Officer in Laos, 1962–1964."** *Studies in Intelligence* 47, no. 1 (2003): 1–17. Originally UNCLASSIFIED.

Richard L. Holm was among the first paramilitary officers to arrive in Laos in January 1962, joining three other experienced officers with similar service elsewhere in Asia dating to the early 1950s. Charged with supporting the Royal Lao Army in its fight against the communist Pathet Lao then supported by North Vietnam, CIA officers collaborated with US Agency for International Development workers assisting different tribal and ethnic groups. Holm and his colleagues focused on the ethnically distinct Hmong tribes of northern Laos, forming militia units and road-watch teams of 15 to 100 members for collecting intelligence and contesting North Vietnamese use of the Ho Chi Minh Trail through eastern Laos to Cambodia and South Vietnam.

Meanwhile, CIA in Laos, 1954–74

McCann, Frederic. **"Gathering Intelligence in Laos in 1968."** *Studies in Intelligence* 49, no. 1 (2005): 27–31. Originally UNCLASSIFIED.

Since 1947, human intelligence collection has been a core CIA mission, conducted worldwide by the officers of the Directorate of Operations during times of war and peace, wherever and whenever the president directs. Agency officer Fredric McCann performed this task in Laos in 1968, interviewing refugees and deserters from the communist Pathet Lao, collecting information that, once analyzed, would provide crucial intelligence to policymakers seeking to develop sound policies for Southeast Asia. McCann's information would supplement collection already obtained through the paramilitary operations the CIA had initiated years before in the region, providing insights into the size, capabilities, and structure of those enemy forces facing CIA and its Laotian and Hmong allies.

Petchell, Robert A. **"Cash on Delivery."** *Studies in Intelligence* 17, no. 3 (1973): 1–7. Originally SECRET—Released in part.

Laotian or Hmong road-watch teams and irregular units with CIA-developed aerial and ground technical collection systems provided vital insights on communist activities in Laos and the movement of troops and supplies down the Ho Chi Minh Trail into South Vietnam. Often, however, weather, mechanical failure, or the unwillingness of the teams to get close to sizable enemy forces frustrated these collection attempts. North Vietnamese soldiers possessed much better and higher quality intelligence, if only they could be captured or convinced to surrender. One CIA operations officer, who worked with Hmong tribesmen organized into special Paramilitary Team Operations units in the southern Laotian Saravane Province and Bolovens Plateau areas, recalls his experiences there. Organized into well-armed groups of about 12 men, the teams worked in the field for two to three months at a time without close supervision, searching for solitary NVA soldiers to "snatch" for intelligence collection purposes.

Stockinger, Edwin K. **"Five Weeks at Phalane."** *Studies in Intelligence* 17, no. 1 (1973): 11–19. Originally SECRET//NOFORN—Released in part.

The offensive by the Army of the Republic of South Vietnam (ARVN) into Laos in February and March 1971, named Operation Lam Son 719, had the twin objectives of cutting the Ho Chi Minh Trail at the vital Route 9 crossroads at Tchepone, while also demonstrating the success of the ongoing "Vietnamization" program aimed at turning the war over to South Vietnam as American troop withdrawals accelerated. South Vietnamese units numbering some 15,000 men initially made good progress against light opposition, but within two weeks, five North Vietnamese divisions totaling 40,000 troops counterattacked, prompting a panicked ARVN retreat back into South Vietnam by the end of March. All sides claimed victory. The history books, however, often say little about the aftermath of Lam Son 719, especially as it played out in Laos. After repulsing the ARVN invasion, NVA units continued attacks to the west toward Savannaket on the Mekong River on the Thai-Laotian border with the goal of cutting the Laotian panhandle in two and permanently securing the Ho Chi Minh

Meanwhile, CIA in Laos, 1954–74

Trail. In the path of this advance along Route 9 lay the village of Muang Phalane, a small district capital and market town that served as a forward operating base for two battalions of CIA-lead Lao paramilitary forces.

Absher, Kenneth Michael. **"John Kearns and the Cold War in Laos."** *Studies in Intelligence* 46, no. 4 (2002): 45–54. Originally SECRET//NOFORN—Released in part.

Seventeen CIA officers and one member of the CIA's predecessor organization—the Office of Strategic Services—lost their lives in service to the nation in the wars in Southeast Asia between September 1945 and July 1976. Told here is "the story of one of CIA's silent heroes, honored by a star on the Memorial Wall," operations officer John Kearns, killed in combat action against the North Vietnamese in December 1972. Like many of his Directorate of Operations colleagues, Kearns served for several years in the US Army Special Forces in Vietnam before joining the CIA. In June 1969, he arrived in Laos as a paramilitary operations officer to direct regular Lao forces, intelligence teams conducting harassing, and interdiction raids against North Vietnamese forces along the Ho Chi Minh Trail. When the communists launched their Easter Offensive in South Vietnam in March 1972, the interdiction and intelligence collection efforts of CIA officers in Laos grew in importance as ever-increasing numbers of communist troops and supplies moved down the Trail. Kearns suffered fatal wounds in a mortar attack near Pak Song on 15 December 1972. He was posthumously awarded the CIA Intelligence Star for his courage and sacrifice.

Postwar Reflections

Bunker, Ellsworth. **"Vietnam in Retrospect."** *Studies in Intelligence* 18, no. 1 (1974): 41–47. Originally CONFIDENTIAL—Released in full.

On 11 December 1973, former US Ambassador to South Vietnam Ellsworth Bunker delivered this address to the CIA workforce at its Langley, Virginia, headquarters. The last US military personnel had left South Vietnam the previous March, in keeping with the peace accords signed in Paris in January of that year. Yet as Bunker noted, the end of the conflict was still nowhere in sight, confiding that "the war's fundamental issue remains unresolved." Nonetheless, the ambassador took the occasion to highlight the contributions CIA had made during the conflict noting, "The role of the Agency in Vietnam was indispensable, both in waging the war and in the negotiations leading to a settlement."

Ford, Harold P. **"Why CIA Analysts Were So Doubtful About Vietnam."** *Studies in Intelligence* 40, no. 2 (1996): 43–53. Originally UNCLASSIFIED.

CIA analysts, as Harold Ford notes, had a well-documented and well-known reputation for skepticism concerning "official pronouncements about the Vietnam war" and consistently remained "fairly pessimistic about the outlook for 'light at the end of the tunnel'." While qualifying that not all analysts always thought alike, and that their views often differed from Agency operations officers in Southeast Asia who had mixed

Postwar Reflections

views on the war, finished intelligence "maintained definitely pessimistic, skeptical tones over the years." Concluding that "the war's outcome justified many of the CIA's analysts' doubts and warnings," it is less well known why such doubts existed, especially given the CIA's central role in advising policymakers on how best to assist South Vietnam.

Allen, George W. **"Intelligence in Small Wars."** *Studies in Intelligence* 35, no. 4 (1991): 19–27. Originally UNCLASSIFIED.

George W. Allen served as an analyst during much of the Vietnam War in the United States and in Saigon. He noted in a 1991 address, "The American intelligence experience in Vietnam included its entire professional repertoire, some facets reasonably well performed, some embarrassingly flawed." However controversial the war remained when Allen spoke 16 years after the fall of South Vietnam, he noted that the oft-spoken "credo 'no more Vietnams'" reflected "wishful thinking." The United States would face future Vietnams and when this inevitable happenstance occurred, he asserted, "Timely and comprehensive intelligence will be needed" lest "policymakers are handicapped" and "fail to act appropriately."

Ford, Harold P. **"Thoughts Engendered by Robert McNamara's 'In Retrospect'."** *Studies in Intelligence* 39, no. 1 (1995): 95–109. Originally UNCLASSIFIED.

In 1995, 20 years after the fall of South Vietnam, former Secretary of Defense Robert S. McNamara (in office 1961–1968) published a memoir of his time in the Pentagon under Presidents John Kennedy and Lyndon Johnson entitled In Retrospect: The Tragedy and Lessons of Vietnam. *Remembered as a staunch Cold War warrior and advocate of committing sizable numbers of US ground forces to the war, especially during 1965–1966, McNamara's 1995 admission of having had early doubts and now a troubled conscience about the role the US played in the wars in Southeast Asia, and that "he and his colleagues were wrong, terribly wrong," caused a firestorm. CIA's Harold Ford, while counted among the many critics, noted that McNamara's "accounting of history is ambiguous, debatable, and, above all selective." Instead of joining in the chorus of criticism, however, Ford focused here on what the secretary said about the CIA's role in the war and how it affected his thinking.*

Hathaway, Robert M. **"Richard Helms as DCI."** *Studies in Intelligence* 37, no. 4 (1993): 33–40. Originally SECRET—Released in full.

The Director of Central Intelligence had a unique role during the wars in Southeast Asia as the primary intelligence adviser to the president—and, as a result, to the nation's top policymakers and military leaders. The job could prove difficult as circumstances and personalities changed with each presidential administration. As Hathaway relates here, Richard Helms, a career intelligence officer, served as DCI for Lyndon Johnson and Richard M. Nixon from 1966 until 1973, earning a position of trust and influence with the former, but never overcoming the distrust of the latter. To Johnson, Helms "kept the game honest." Yet as Hathaway notes, while Johnson valued Helms, he largely ignored CIA's pessimistic analyses that conflicted with the optimistic line the White House took on the progress of the wars in Vietnam and

Postwar Reflections

elsewhere in Southeast Asia. As rocky as it may have been at times, Hathaway further notes, the LBJ years "seemed almost a golden era" of White House–CIA relations compared with what followed. The article is an excerpt from a book-length study of Helms, which has since been released with redactions. It is available in the FOIA Electronic Reading Room under Historical Collections/Richard Helms Collection.

Ford, Harold P. **"William Colby: Retrospect."** *Studies in Intelligence* 40, no. 1 (1996): 1–5. Originally UNCLASSIFIED.

William E. Colby succeeded Richard Helms as DCI to President Richard Nixon and to President Gerald Ford—a tumultuous tenure running from May 1973 until January 1976. Colby navigated CIA through times of significant changes in US domestic and foreign affairs to include the resignation of a president, the fall of South Vietnam, and the unprecedented public, media, and congressional scrutiny of CIA over real and alleged wrongdoing and illegal activities that resulted in wholesale changes in oversight and accountability. As Harold Ford writes, early on as DCI, Colby "enjoyed some success in illustrating his managerial skills, his powers of initiative, and—most of all—his unique confidence that the times called for a new, more open CIA."

Lewis, Anthony Marc. **"Re-examining Our Perceptions on Vietnam."** *Studies in Intelligence* 17, no. 4 (1973): 1–62. Original SECRET—Released in full.

Even before the fall of the Republic of South Vietnam to communist forces in April 1975, intelligence officers and academics began to search for enduring lessons from the decades of US involvement. Senior CIA career analyst Anthony Marc Lewis, educated as a political scientist, suggested that US policies were not as successful as they could have been due to the inability of Americans at all levels, especially within the CIA, "to see 'the world of the Vietnamese' as the Vietnamese do." Lewis recommended a future emphasis on analytical training that assured recognition of "cultural blinders" such as he claimed had unconsciously affected CIA analysis.

Laurie, Clayton. **"Intelligence in Public Literature, Takes on Intelligence and the Vietnam War"**—a review essay of *Vietnam: The History of an Unwinnable War, 1945–1975*, by John Prados; *Why Vietnam Matters: An Eyewitness Account of Lessons Not Learned*, by Rufus Phillips; and *This Time We Win: Revisiting the Tet Offensive*, by James S. Robbins." *Studies in Intelligence* 55, no. 2 (2011): 73–77. Originally UNCLASSIFIED.

In this review essay concerning three books published during the period 2008–2010, CIA historian Clayton Laurie opens by recalling President John F. Kennedy's question of two members of a factfinding team who offered different and opposing assessments of US progress in Vietnam in 1963: "The two of you did visit the same country, didn't you?" Laurie suggests that readers of these three books seeking a better understanding of the CIA's role in Southeast Asia and the lessons of that conflict for today may well ask a similar question. Nearly 40 years after the end of the US involvement, after the publication of a score of histories describing CIA activities during that time, and after the declassification of thousands of documents, opinions regarding Agency failures and accomplishments remain far apart, as do the authors' interpretations of how the experiences of Vietnam apply to the conflicts of today.

Consolidated List of Cited Articles and Other Resources

Absher, Kenneth Michael. "John Kearns and the Cold War in Laos." *Studies in Intelligence* 46, no. 4 (2002): 45–54. Originally SECRET//NOFORN—Released in part.

Ahern, Thomas L. Jr. "The CIA and the Government of Ngo Dinh Diem." *Studies in Intelligence* 37, no. 4 (1993): 41–51. Originally SECRET—Released in part.

Allen, George W. "Covering Coups in Saigon." *Studies in Intelligence* 33, no. 4 (1989): 57–61. Originally SECRET—Released in part.

Allen, George W. "Intelligence in Small Wars." *Studies in Intelligence* 35, no. 4 (1991): 19–27. Originally UNCLASSIFIED.

Atkins, Merle, Kenneth C. Fuller, and Bruce Smith. "'Rolling Thunder' and Bomb Damage to Bridges." *Studies in Intelligence* 13, no. 4 (1969): 1–9. Originally SECRET//NOFORN—Released in full.

Bunker, Ellsworth. "Vietnam in Retrospect." *Studies in Intelligence* 18, no. 1 (1974): 41–47. Originally CONFIDENTIAL—Released in full.

Castle, Timothy. "From the Bay of Pigs to Laos—Operation MILLPOND: The Beginning of a Distant Covert War." *Studies in Intelligence*, 59, no. 2 (2015): 1–16. Originally UNCLASSIFIED.

Elkes, Martin C. "The LAMS Story." *Studies in Intelligence* 19, no. 2 (1975): 29–34. Originally SECRET—Released in part.

Finlayson, Andrew R. "The Tay Ninh Provincial Reconnaissance Unit and Its Role in the Phoenix Program, 1969–70." *Studies in Intelligence* 51, no. 2 (2007): 59–69. Originally UNCLASSIFIED.

Ford, Harold P. "The US Decision to Go Big in Vietnam." *Studies in Intelligence* 29, no. 1 (1985): 1–15. Originally SECRET//NOFORN—Released in full.

———, "Thoughts Engendered by Robert McNamara's In Retrospect." *Studies in Intelligence* 39, no. 1 (1995): 95–109. Originally UNCLASSIFIED.

———, "Why CIA Analysts Were So Doubtful About Vietnam." *Studies in Intelligence* 40, no. 2 (1996): 43–53. Originally UNCLASSIFIED.

———, "William Colby: Retrospect." *Studies in Intelligence* 40, no. 1 (1996): 1–5. Originally UNCLASSIFIED.

Hall, Arthur B. "Landscape Analysis." *Studies in Intelligence* 11, no. 3 (1967): 65–75. Originally SECRET//NOFORN—Released in full.

Hartness, William M. "Aspects of Counterinsurgency Intelligence." *Studies in Intelligence* 7, no. 4 (1963): 71–83. Originally CONFIDENTIAL—Released in full.

Hathaway, Robert M. "Richard Helms as DCI." *Studies in Intelligence* 37, no. 4 (1993): 33–40. Originally SECRET—Released in full.

Holm, Richard L. "Recollections of a Case Officer in Laos, 1962–1964." *Studies in Intelligence* 47, no. 1 (2003): 1–17. Originally UNCLASSIFIED.

Kitchens, Allen H. "Crisis and Intelligence: Two Case Studies [Tet and Iran]." *Studies in Intelligence* 28, No. 3 (1984): 71–78. Originally UNCLASSIFIED.

Laurie, Clayton. "Intelligence in Public Literature, Takes on Intelligence and the Vietnam War"—a review essay of *Vietnam: The History of an Unwinnable War, 1945–1975*, by John Prados; *Why Vietnam Matters: An Eyewitness Account of Lessons Not Learned*, by Rufus Phillips; *This Time We Win: Revisiting the Tet Offensive*, by James S. Robbins. *Studies in Intelligence* 55, no. 2 (2011): 73–77. Originally UNCLASSIFIED.

Leary, William M. "CIA Air Operations in Laos, 1955–1974." *Studies in Intelligence* 42, no. 2 (1998): 71–86. Originally UNCLASSIFIED.

Leidesdorf, Titus. "The Vietnamese as Operational Target." *Studies in Intelligence* 12, no. 4 (1968): 57–71. Originally SECRET—Released in full.

LePage, Jean-Marc and Elie Tenenbaum. "French and American Intelligence Relations During the First Indochina War, 1950–1954." *Studies in Intelligence* 55, no. 3 (2011): 19–27. Originally UNCLASSIFIED.

Lewis, Anthony Marc. "Re-examining Our Perceptions on Vietnam." *Studies in Intelligence* 17, no. 4 (1973): 1–62. Original SECRET—Released in full.

Linder, James C. "The Fall of Lima Site 85." *Studies in Intelligence* 38, no. 4 (1994): 43–52. Originally UNCLASSIFIED and reprinted with updating editor's note and new afterword in *Studies in Intelligence* 59, no. 1 (March 2015).

Mark, David, "The Mayaguez Rescue Operation Revisited." *Studies in Intelligence* 23, no. 2 (1979): 29–32. Originally SECRET//NOFORN—Released in full.

Matthias, Willard C. "How Three Estimates Went Wrong." *Studies in Intelligence* 12, no. 1 (1968): 27–38. Originally SECRET//NOFORN—Released in part.

Maximov, William J. and Edward Scrutchings. "The Metal Traces Test." *Studies in Intelligence* 11, no. 4 (1967): 37–44. Originally CONFIDENTIAL//NOFORN—Released in full.

McCann, Frederic. "Gathering Intelligence in Laos in 1968." *Studies in Intelligence* 49, no. 1 (2005): 27–31. Originally UNCLASSIFIED.

Palmer, Gen. Bruce. "US Intelligence and Vietnam." *Studies in Intelligence* 28, no. 5 (Special Issue, 1984). Originally SECRET//NOFORN—Released in part.

Petchell, Robert A. "Cash on Delivery." *Studies in Intelligence* 17, no. 3 (1973): 1–7. Originally SECRET—Released in part.

Peterson, Gordon I. and David C. Taylor. "A Shield and Sword: Intelligence Support to Communications with US POWs in Vietnam." *Studies in Intelligence* 60, no. 1 (2016): 1–16. Originally UNCLASSIFIED.

Pribbenow, Merle L. "The Man in the Snow White Cell." *Studies in Intelligence* 48, no. 1 (2004): 59–69. Originally UNCLASSIFIED.

Puchalla, Edward F. "Communist Defense Against Aerial Surveillance in Southeast Asia." *Studies in Intelligence* 14, no. 2 (1970): 31–78. Originally SECRET// NOFORN—Released in full.

Schiattareggia, M. H. "Counterintelligence in Counter-Guerrilla Operations." *Studies in Intelligence* 6, no. 3 (1962): 1–24. Originally SECRET—Released in full and reprinted in Studies in Intelligence 57, no. 2 (2013): 39–63.

Schwarzchild, Edward T. "The Assessment of Insurgency." *Studies in Intelligence* 7, no. 4 (1963): 85–89. Originally SECRET—Released in full.

Sinclair, Robert, "One Intelligence Analyst Remembers Another: A Review of *Who the Hell Are We Fighting?—The Story of Sam Adams and the Vietnam Intelligence Wars.*" *Studies in Intelligence* 50, no. 4 (2006): 1–9. Originally UNCLASSIFIED.

Smith, Russell Jack. "Intelligence Production During the Helms Regime." *Studies in Intelligence* 39, no. 4 (1995): 93–102. Originally SECRET—Released in part.

Steinmeyer, Walter. "The Intelligence Role in Counterinsurgency." *Studies in Intelligence* 9, no. 4 (1965): 57–63. Originally SECRET—Released in full and reprinted in *Studies in Intelligence* 59, no. 4 (December 2015). Steinmeyer is a penname for a former senior operations officer, Theodore Shackley.

Stockinger, Edwin K. "Five Weeks at Phalane." *Studies in Intelligence* 17, no. 1 (1973): 11–19. Originally SECRET//NOFORN—Released in part.

Swift, Carleton A., Richard D. Kovar, and Russell J. Bowen. "Intelligence in Recent Public Literature: *Why Vietnam? Prelude to America's Albatross.*" *Studies in Intelligence* 25, no. 2 (1981): 99–116. Originally UNCLASSIFIED.

Tidwell, William A. "A New Kind of Air Targeting." *Studies in Intelligence* 11, no. 1 (1967): 55–60. Originally CONFIDENTIAL//NOFORN—Released in full.

Other References:

Hathaway, Robert M. and Russell Jack Smith, *Richard Helms as Director of Central Intelligence*. Available at http://www.foia.cia.gov/document/richard-helms-director-central-intelligence-robert-m-hathaway-and-russell-jack-smith.

Robarge, David. *John McCone as Director of Central Intelligence, 1961–65.* Available at http://www.foia.cia.gov/collection/john-mccone-director-central-intelligence-1961-1965. Originally SECRET//NOFORN—Released in part.

———, Archangel: *CIA's Supersonic A-12 Reconnaissance Aircraft.* Available at http://www.cia.gov/library/center-for-the-study-of-intelligence/csi-publications/books-and-monographs/a-12/index.html

Air America: *Holding Up the Airman's Bond.* CIA Historical Documents Collection. Available at http://www.foia.cia.gov/collection/air-america-upholding-airmens-bond.

The National Intelligence Council Vietnam Collection of Estimates and Papers. Available at http://www.foia.cia.gov/collection/vietnam-collection.

The Vietnam Histories of Thomas L. Ahern, Jr. Available at http://www.foia.cia.gov/collection/vietnam-histories.

The Collection of Presidential Briefing Products from 1961 to 1969. Available at http://www.foia.cia.gov/collection/PDBs.

www.ingramcontent.com/pod-product-compliance
Lightning Source LLC
Chambersburg PA
CBHW081524040426

42447CB00013B/3332

9 781839 314148